The
SPIRITUAL PRACTICES
of
RUꝂI

"Instead of recycling old information, Will Johnson brings new light to the understanding of Rumi with this book. This is how we can bring Rumi to our life rather than bury him in scholarly libraries."

Nevit O. Ergin, translator of Rumi's *Divan-i Kebir*

"In these most troubled of times, Johnson makes available for any and all the secret of beholding the divine in sacred friendship. This makes for sensitive and intriguing reading that goes right to your heart."

José Argüelles, author of *Time and the Technosphere:
The Law of Time in Human Affairs*

The
SPIRITUAL PRACTICES
of
RUMI

Radical Techniques for
Beholding the Divine

WILL JOHNSON

Inner Traditions
Rochester, Vermont

Inner Traditions
One Park Street
Rochester, Vermont 05767
www.InnerTraditions.com

Originally published in 2003 under the title *Rumi: Gazing at the Beloved*
First paperback edition published in 2007 under the title *The Spiritual Practices of Rumi*

The author wishes to thank the following people and companies for granting him permission to reprint copyrighted material:

Coleman Barks, James Cowan, Nevit O. Ergin, Shahram Shiva, and Jonathan Star for permission to use their copyrighted translations of Rumi's poetry.

Suzin Green for permission to use a poem from her CD *Hearts on Fire,* which is reprinted in chapter 8.

Daniel Ladinsky for permission to reprint a poem that originally appeared in *I Heard God Laughing, Renderings of Hafiz,* copyright Daniel Ladinsky 1999, published by Sufism Reoriented, Walnut Creek, California 94595.

Jeremy P. Tarcher for permission to quote passages from *The Way of Passion* by Andrew Harvey, 1994.

Sounds True for permission to quote passages from *The Song of the Sun* by Andrew Harvey, 1999.

Shambhala Publications for permission to quote passages from *Signs of the Unseen* by W. M. Thackston, Jr., 1994, *I Am Wind, You Are Fire* by Annemarie Schimmel, 1992, and *Teachings of Rumi* by Andrew Harvey, 1999.

Ice Nine Publishing Company for permission to use the lyric from the song "Casey Jones" by Robert Hunter.

Library of Congress Cataloging-in-Publication Data
Johnson, Will, 1946–
  [Rumi, gazing at the beloved]
  The spiritual practices of Rumi : radical techniques for beholding the divine / Will Johnson.—2nd ed.
      p. cm.
  Originally published under the title: Rumi, gazing at the beloved. 2003.
  Includes bibliographical references.
  ISBN-13: 978-1-59477-200-9 (pbk.)
  ISBN-10: 1-59477-200-2 (pbk.)
  1. Jalal al-Din Rumi, Maulana, 1207–1273. 2. God (Islam)—Worship and love. 3. Spiritual life—Islam. 4. Sufism—Doctrines. I. Title.
  BP189.7.M42J65 2007
  297.4'46—dc22

                                                                          2007021557

Printed and bound in the United States at McNaughton & Gunn

10 9 8 7 6 5 4 3 2 1

Text design and layout by Priscilla Baker
This book was typeset in Sabon with Centaur as the display typeface

This book is dedicated to the tribe of gazers—
past, present, and future—
some of whom I've met,
all of whom are my family.

Contents

Part III. Alone Together

Introduction

*J*ust as archers fix their gaze upon a distant target before loosing the strings of their bows and sending their arrows flying, so do lovers of God fix their gaze on the face of God, each releasing the soul so it too can fly toward its target where it celebrates its homecoming. All spiritual paths teach us that if we want to find God, then we need to turn directly toward God, come face-to-face with the energies of the Divine, and then surrender to whatever begins to occur as a result of the impact that such an encounter creates in our lives. But where do we turn? And where exactly is it that we find the face of the Divine? Is it everywhere? Or in one particular location only? And can perhaps a particular location, a particular face, serve as the doorway to the face of God?

One way to look upon the face of God is to create an image of God, either a painting or a sculpture, and then gaze at the image for an extended period of time. This practice can be found in the Greek Orthodox church where icons of saints and personages from the Bible are the only companions that monks and nuns take with them into the isolation of their cells during long periods of retreat. When one fixes his or her entire attention on these images over long hours and days, the images may come to life and enter into animated dialogue with the practitioner. Many devout Hindus create personal shrines in their homes and temples in which images of a god or goddess serve as the means for personal dialogue with the Divine. It is said that the eyes of these images are the most important of all the facial features, for by creating eye contact with the image a devotee achieves *darshan,* a sanskrit word meaning "seeing and being seen by God."

Most of our spiritual traditions tell us that, as humans, we are miniature reflections of God and that we have been created in God's image. If this is so, then it would follow that a more direct way to look upon the face of God would be to sit and gaze at an actual person, a real flesh-and-blood human. If he or she will sit and hold your gaze in return, something begins to transpire between the two of you. If you can truly see another and be seen by the other, you begin to see that he or she is an embodiment of the Divine, and you begin to feel that you are as well.

In India, darshan often occurs in formal settings between teachers and their students. Teachers may sit at the front of a room, perhaps on a slightly raised dais so that no one's view will be obstructed. They may sit silently, pouring out their gazing, inviting students to meet their eyes and to hold contact with their gaze. This contact allows the Divine to enter their students' awareness. In the words of Ramana Maharshi, one of the great Indian teachers of the twentieth century and one of the great givers of darshan, "When the eyes of the student meet the gaze of the teacher, words of instruction are no longer necessary."

Why gazing at another person and having him or her hold your gaze in return can open both participants to a direct experience of the Divine is a mystery that this book will examine and attempt to explain. All of us, whether we're consciously aware of it or not, know about this practice from a very early age. Schoolchildren will often enter into staring contests during which their conventional experience of self is momentarily suspended to accommodate the new and unusual energies that the visual contact between them generates. A common response to the dramatic shift in awareness that prolonged eye contact triggers is to burst into laughter, and so the contest ends with both of the children being the true winners, with smiles on their faces.

As we mature and need to become strong individuals, separate from the whole, we tend to avoid eye contact when we speak to others, for if we did hold the other's gaze we might find it difficult to remain focused on the information that we're trying to convey, melting instead into a shared sense of wordless union with the person to whom we're speaking. Only when real love forms the basis of our communication with another do we find it more natural to hold and soften into our partner's gaze.

Because the eyes are universally acknowledged to be the windows to the soul, when we hold the gaze of another, we hold and cradle his or her soul. This most intimate of acts is reserved as a privilege for people who love and trust one another. Newborn children are natural adepts at the practice and are often able to draw their parents into gazing at them for long periods of time. People newly in love may find that they automatically fall into gazing at each other as a natural expression of the love that they feel. In fact, this unintentional and spontaneous dissolving into the eyes of the other is often the signal that, at long last, they have finally found the beloved for whom they've been searching. When describing this newfound love, people will often rejoice that, finally, they have met someone who truly sees them as they are.

When eye contact between two people is initiated and maintained, an invisible energetic circuit is established between the two participants, dissolving the barriers that ordinarily separate them from each other, drawing them ever closer into a shared awareness of union. This experience of union is always pervaded by the feeling tone of love, just as the experience of separation from others, as well as from the larger world we inhabit, tends to breed feelings of fear and alienation. However, we live in a culture that worships the individual and that is embarrassed by joint forays into the Divine, into the great ground of being that is our heritage and true birthright as humans on this planet. In our culture, this most natural of actions, the holding of the gaze between two people, is taboo. And, yet, how tragic it is that we turn away from this heritage, forfeiting our birthright in an act of fear.

In the area of Vancouver Island on which I live, the elders of the Cowichan tribe speak of the "disease of the eye." They describe this condition as what occurs when we're walking down the road and avert our gaze when we pass by other humans instead of looking at them directly in the eye, acknowledging them as God's noble creatures, seeing them and being seen by them. This act of aversion is seen as a turning away from a moment of grace and, ultimately, constitutes a turning away not just from the other person, but from ourselves as well, for the blessings of holding the gaze of other humans cure the disease of the eye and leave us feeling whole.

Isn't it true that, if we happen to look into the eyes of a stranger at the same moment the stranger is looking into ours, we'll usually avert our gaze? Our fear won't permit us to maintain the contact that our interest in each other has spawned. By choosing fear in this way, we perpetuate our notions of separation and exclusion and continue on our way. If we're able to look into another person's eyes and hold his or her gaze, however, a whole other set of conclusions reveals itself. In just a few minutes' time our conventional boundaries begin to soften, losing their hard edge of distinction and opacity. The energy fields of our bodies, which people with particularly sensitive vision can perceive as auras, slowly begin to merge, the one flowing into and out of the other.

Once this connection has been established, our communication deepens, and the feeling tone of the encounter begins to shift dramatically. Like two objects that have entered into a whirlpool and are together drawn down inexorably to its common source, our experiences of our personal self and of the other gradually merge and, at a very deep level, may even become indistinguishable. We enter into darshan together. Like iron filings being drawn to a powerful magnetic source, we experience ourselves as being ineluctably drawn closer to a shared feeling of union, relatedness, and love. Where formerly we were two separate beings, we join together through the practice and become something that neither of us could quite be on our own. When hydrogen comes into the presence of oxygen, suddenly there's water. Likewise, through such a meeting, two people lose their sense of separateness and drown together in the waters of love and union.

Looking into another's eyes and holding his or her gaze need not be just a pastime of schoolchildren or the privilege of new lovers or parents of newborns. It represents a practice capable of taking the participants to the deepest feelings and the purest awareness of self that are available to a human being. Some would call this pure awareness God, and down through the ages this practice has spontaneously appeared and reappeared wherever lovers of God, lovers of the ultimate source of their own being, have come together and truly met one another. The quintessential Hindu lovers, Radha and Krishna, are often depicted as sitting silently, raptly gazing at each other, surrounded by a luminous glow for all to see. Is the light that surrounds their bodies a function of their high spiritual station, or could it be the natural result of a love that leaves them no option but to gaze at each other with adoration?

More recently, a number of modern spiritual teachers have incorporated eye gazing into the body of their practices as a direct means to attain realization of the most profound spiritual truths that, all too often, remain obscured from our vision. Oscar Ichazo, a Chilean-born Sufi teacher, has developed a practice called *traspasso,* in which students sit across from each other and hold each other's gaze. The teachings of tantra that are proliferating in the West often include periods of eye gazing between the couple who are entering into the tantric ritual. Another story comes out of the tradition of Zen Buddhism. During the long *sesshins,* or practice periods, participants may meditate for up to sixteen hours a day for as much as a week at a time or longer. It is customary for the students to enter into the *zendo* in single file, walk around its perimeter until they come to a cushion that is placed on the floor, sit down on the cushion with their backs to the center of the room, facing the wall, and begin their meditation. In this way, a ring of students lines the circumference of the meditation hall with their backs to one another. One day, however, a Japanese teacher decided to experiment with the format and instructed everyone to turn around, away from the wall, and sit facing the center of the room. Thus, the students naturally encountered the gaze of other students sitting directly across the room from them, and the teacher observed that spiritual realization began occurring much more rapidly through this kind of direct human connection. Joko Beck, a contemporary Zen teacher, includes periods of eye gazing in her sesshins.

For me, however, the most extraordinary account of the practice of eye gazing can be traced to the meeting that occurred in Konya, Turkey, in 1244 between the renowned poet, Sufi teacher, and originator of the dance of the whirling dervish, Jalaluddin Rumi, and a wandering seeker named Shams-i Tabriz. Out of the many recorded stories and traditions of darshan, it is the story of this grand and divine spiritual love affair that I have chosen to focus on in this book as a way of presenting and explaining the practice of gazing at the beloved, and there are several reasons for my doing this.

In the first place, I feel deeply drawn to the story of Rumi and Shams because both Rumi's ecstatic expression of his understanding through the medium of words and his great, uninhibited love for wild music and dancing are dear to my heart and closely parallel my own path of practices. It is also one of the most well documented encounters of this kind that exists, although such a statement may come as a surprise to practitioners of Sufism for whom the relationship between Rumi and Shams has always been enshrouded in secrecy and presented as a profound mystery. In truth, very little of what actually transpired between these two great friends has ever been recorded, and Rumi himself was reluctant ever to speak directly about the practices that he and Shams were engaged in during their long retreats.

However, out of the explosion that occurred through Rumi's encounter with Shams, Rumi began spontaneously writing some of the most splendorous poetry about the soul's return to God that has ever been composed, and his writings are voluminous. If you read the poetry with an eye to the practices that will be presented in this book, you quickly realize that allusions to the practice of gazing at the beloved—and even explicit instructions and descriptions of it—are *everywhere*. These clues trail through Rumi's poetry and discourses like shiny pebbles that we drop along an unmarked path in a forest to help us find our way back home. Indeed, the practice of gazing at the beloved truly signals a great homecoming for the participants who are fortunate enough to have found one another.

It is my sincere hope that this book will serve, at least partially, to clear up the 750-year-old mystery about what Rumi and Shams were actually doing behind the closed doors of their retreat room. From all accounts, what the two were doing together was nothing less than dying into love, and such an experience is rightly spoken of as a mystery. But wouldn't it be wonderful to participate ourselves in the practices that let them grow wings and fly toward the sun? Wouldn't it be wonderful if we, too, could grow those wings and set out ourselves on this greatest of journeys?

Some mysteries are like puzzles or riddles that the discerning eye and mind can recognize, unravel, piece together, and then solve. Other mysteries (as the mystery of dying into love) are simply to be entered into, marveled over, and surrendered to with no hope whatsoever of ever conquering or solving them. In fact, the only way of truly understanding such a mystery is instead through letting ourselves be completely conquered and dissolved by it. Let's see if we can solve the mystery of what Rumi and Shams were actually doing together so that we too can enter into the great mystery that can never be solved.

As preparation for writing this book, I have feasted on Rumi's poetry and discourses, and what a feast it has proven to be! His words are like the most resplendent and freshly set banquet table, large enough for all of us to sit at, and they come with a personally engraved invitation for us to take a seat and savor the most sublime foods and wines imaginable. It is said that Rumi is currently the most popular and widely read poet in the Western world. As for the most exquisite of foods, readers find that, once they develop a taste for what he's offering, they want to return again and again to feast anew. How wonderful it is that people in the West are developing a palate for these odes and ravings, these extraordinary expressions of our need to search for the face of God, to find that face, and to dissolve ourselves completely into that face.

Passages from Rumi's writings will liberally populate the pages ahead of you and serve as illustrations for the presentation of these practices. If the authorship of a passage is not otherwise ascribed, then the text has been gleaned from one of the pages of Rumi's poetry or discourses.

In closing this Introduction, and in preparation for the adventure that lies ahead, I'd like to acknowledge all of the lovers of Rumi who, like me, have gained from his words both encouragement for their own practices and the great enjoyment that comes from being in the presence of the highest artistry. It is one thing, however, to enjoy the words. It is another to enter into the experience to which the poetry alludes and out of which it was born, and this is my intention for the readers of this book. As our journey together begins, I'd like to offer as an appetizer to the banquet that awaits us these lines of Rumi's, taken from several of his poems and put together here:

> Look at me. Look at me.
> Look at me, even just once, with those drunken
>   eyes.
> I've become crazy, insane
> From your drunken eyes.
> Amazing trees
> Grow from one seed with your look.
> Open your eyes
> And look at me carefully.
> If you have the eyes, look and see.

PART I

Best of Friends

Trouble with you
Is the trouble with me.
Got two good eyes,
But we still don't see.

"Casey Jones," Robert Hunter
and the Grateful Dead

Jalaluddin and Shams

Who were these two men, these two great friends? So inebriated in soul, and yet so sober in body, they somehow managed to find each other, and the sparks from the contact of their interaction erupted into a fire that, as a moth to a flame, drew God to Earth. And what were they doing together behind the closed doors of their retreat room, these two grown men, so deeply beloved of each other? The one had searched his entire life for someone to pour himself into, the other was so receptive that he was willing to have his life turned completely upside down, not caring what anyone said, not caring about the appearances of their relationship. This friendship, to those who saw only with the eyes of this world, must have looked utterly mystifying. Shams was like a key to Jalaluddin's lock, and through their meeting whole universes of experience were opened, literally before their eyes. A key on its own is not of much value, and the lock of even the most beautiful door will rust over time if it's not opened.

Of the two, we know much more about Jalaluddin than we do

about Shams. Jalaluddin was born into a family of religious scholars and seekers in what is now Afghanistan but, like a Jew fleeing Germany in the 1930s, was forced to leave his homeland at an early age to escape the Mongol battalions of Genghis Khan that kept advancing ever closer to the horizon of his birthplace. After wandering toward the west for many years and visiting many of the sacred sites of Islam, his father finally settled his family in the town of Konya in present-day Turkey, where he was invited to take up a position as a religious teacher. The area in which they settled was known in those days as the land of Rum, and it is from this geographical designation that Jalaluddin acquired the name by which most of us in the West now know him.

During his family's years of wandering, a number of prominent teachers recognized the great promise and grace that already shone so brightly in Jalaluddin. ("The father is a great lake, but the son is a mighty ocean!" the renowned mystical author Ibn Arabi is reported to have exclaimed after meeting them.) So it was no surprise when, after his father passed away, Jalaluddin took up his position as head of the religious college that his father had created in Konya.

Like many a prudent son thrust too early into the position of leading an established family enterprise, Jalaluddin turned to trusted family associates to help him. In this case, he submitted himself to the teachings and ascetic disciplines of a friend and disciple of his father's, a man named Burhanuddin, who over the next ten years put his young ward through a series of arduous spiritual exercises designed to purify the mind and prepare the body for the demands of his position as spiritual guide and guardian to the townspeople of Konya. By the end of this period of discipleship, Jalaluddin was well prepared to fill the shoes of his father, who had been known in his time as a "king of scholars." Like birds who suddenly come upon a hidden cache of grain, students began flocking to the school of this young teacher who spoke with such eloquence and authority on the traditional teachings of Islam.

Jalaluddin enjoyed the warm intimacy of family life with his wife, who had been his childhood sweetheart, and their two sons. Konya at that time was relatively immune to the Mongol menace, a haven for learning, study, and freedom. Ever more students came to hear the discourses of the young teacher, accepting him as their guiding light. His future, as we would say, looked exceedingly bright.

And then Shams arrived and, in that single moment of meeting, Jalaluddin's world fell apart.

Shams's origins, and his path to the meeting with Jalaluddin, are much more obscure. While it's generally acknowledged that he too came from a family of spiritual practitioners, some scholars view the lineage into which he was born as quite traditional for the times. Others suggest that his forebears were connected to various fringe sects of Sufism whose affiliates experimented with highly unorthodox practices, such as the ingestion of hallucinogenic plants as a sacrament for spiritual unfolding. For these seekers, the desire to attain mystical union with the Divine took precedence over the conventional and more accepted Islamic teachings.

Whatever his background, Shams succeeded in gaining an unsavory reputation throughout the entire Sufi world as a troublemaker and spiritual malcontent. Some thought him mad. Others saw in him an emanation of the divine trickster. Almost everyone experienced him as a pain in the hindquarters of Sufi orthodoxy. He could be extremely derisive toward and contemptuous of any teacher whom he perceived as sacrificing the uncompromising pursuit of mystical realization for displays of false piety. Nor did he endear himself to anyone by suggesting any alternative solutions to the hypocrisy that he perceived to exist all around him. His method appeared to be to complain loudly and bitterly, generally behave badly and make a nuisance of himself, and then move on. So much was he on the move, never settling down in any one place for any length of time, that he earned the epithet Paranda, which means "the winged one" or "the flier."

Shams was not one to hold any personal ambitions of becoming a renowned leader or teacher. He didn't want students. He didn't want recognition. All he wanted was someone to meet him in the fiery dimension of mystical union into which he had fallen, to find someone who was capable of, as he said, "enduring my company." And he burned in his desire to find this one person, someone into whom he could pour himself, someone capable of enduring his heat, containing his blaze, and transforming it into the light of the sun; all this he knew to be his destiny as the word *shams* means "sun" in Persian.

Some accounts tell us that Shams had met Jalaluddin briefly many years before their true encounter. Others suggest that he had passionately beseeched God to direct him to just one good man capable of receiving and merging with the blinding light and energy that were being channeled through his body and soul, and from the depth of his prayers he received an answer to go and seek out Jalaluddin of Konya. Shams was an older man, well into his sixties, when he set out for Konya, and his life had become increasingly lonely and claustrophobic. Like a river in flood season, he needed to spill over his banks, to unite with another in the waters of divine love just once before he passed beyond this world. And he knew he didn't have much time left.

Whatever his motivation, Shams found himself in Konya in December of 1244 where he and Jalaluddin finally came face-to-face, and the dance between them began. Again, different chroniclers have reported different accounts of their initial meeting. Some suggest that Shams caused several of Jalaluddin's sacred books to burst into flame (for how could true knowledge of God be found in books?). Others tell that Shams flippantly tossed Jalaluddin's books into a fountain and then retrieved them for the aghast young teacher—and none were wet. The most widely accepted story of their meeting has Shams posing a trick question to Jalaluddin, with the impact of their dialogue causing Jalaluddin to faint at Shams's feet. When he regained consciousness, he embraced Shams, acknowledged him as the one for whom he too had been yearning for so many years, took him by the hand, and together they went into a room, shut its door, and remained secluded in retreat for several months.

While the last account might most accurately describe what actually occurred between the two great friends, I think it may miss the point somewhat by focusing only on the external particulars of the meeting. Underneath the surface of the reported details of their encounter, far beyond the questions that were asked and the replies that were given, something altogether extraordinary must have transpired between these two men. The experience was so powerful that each had no choice but to throw away, without any hesitation, the current script of their lives and enter together into the most intimate and devastating communion.

Yet another chronicler gives us a hint for what this was, and I feel, of all the stories, it sheds the most light on what actually occurred on that afternoon in the late fall so many years ago. In this account, it is reported that at one point Jalaluddin and Shams remained speechless for several minutes, each of them unable to take his eyes off the other, each burning his gaze into the other and receiving the other's gaze in return. Jalaluddin would later report that, in this extended and silent moment of meeting, he felt his gaze meet the gaze of Shams, and his mind began to melt.

I would like to suggest that, in that glorious moment of meeting soul-to-soul, they spontaneously entered into the practice of gazing at the beloved; that they connected in a way that neither of them had ever experienced before; and that the experience of this initial great dissolving was so powerful, and so obviously revelatory of the greatest truths to which both of them had dedicated their lives, that they could do nothing but go off together, hand in hand, soul in soul, and explore the miracle that had just fallen into their laps. I believe—and the poetry bears witness to this belief—that they continued, behind the closed door of their retreat room, to hold each other's gaze for long periods at a time, relaxing and surrendering into the practice, dissolving together into a shared awareness of the great ground of being, the one universal soul of which their two separate bodies, and all bodies, were but individual manifestations.

Later, Jalaluddin would recount the significance of their meeting with these words:

> Oh, Shams of Tabriz,
> You are both the sea and the pearl,
> And the mystery of your being is the secret of
>   the Creator.
> The first time I saw you
> My soul heard words from your soul,
> And when my heart drank water from your
>   fountain
> It drowned in you,
> And the river swept me away.

Remember that the eyes are universally acknowledged to be the portal to the soul. When Jalaluddin's and Shams's eyes met for that very first time on that afternoon in Konya, their souls began speaking to each other in the silent language of the heart.

When eyes meet in this way, when they truly meet in softness and surrender, the souls of the two gazers begin pouring into each other. The small mind and the limited sense of self of both participants lift like a thinning blanket of fog, and the astonishing warmth of the sun shines suddenly down on the landscape below. The larger sense of self that is revealed, what Jalaluddin calls "the mystery of your being," is truly the one great secret hidden behind the scaffolding of creation. To discover for ourselves the concealed messages of that secret is, for the Sufi, our true challenge as humans. The cold and hardened sorrows of our soul start to melt, just like ice that is exposed to the heat of the sun, and we begin to participate in the watery play of the creative life force itself. The energies of the heart are like a mighty river. The only way truly to explore this river is to throw ourselves in at the deepest end, surrender to the powerful currents that can be felt to animate the waters, and let ourselves be swept away forever downstream.

Elsewhere, Jalaluddin tells us:

> *Look through Shams' eyes*
> *Into the water that is entirely jewels.*

In other words, pass your awareness right through the eyes of your great friend. What you'll find there is an ocean of consciousness in which you can both swim freely, like the most contented fish in the sea. Connect with the divine, watery current that is your common birth-right, and you will realize that this dimension of experience is valuable beyond anything that either of you has ever known.

Ordinarily, this place of meeting, this reconnection back into what Jalaluddin in another poem calls "the origin of your own origin," is kept hidden from view. But all you need for this vision to appear before you is to acquire the eyes to see—and guess what? You already have them! Your two eyes are perfectly good. You simply need to start using them for the purpose for which they were designed. When you let yourself see, when you come face-to-face with your great friend and truly look, with naked openness and relaxation and surrender, then the veil that keeps the magnificence of your birthright hidden from your eyes suddenly lifts. Transported in a heartbeat onto the beach of your soul, you behold the ocean of your origin of origins.

The younger Jalaluddin clearly looked to Shams as his guide and mentor. It was Shams who opened the door of Jalaluddin's heart. It was Shams who understood the mystery that Jalaluddin wanted to penetrate more than anything in the world, and it was Shams who first instructed Jalaluddin in the practice of gazing. Even though Jalaluddin's influence on humanity would ultimately greatly eclipse the influence of Shams, he always acknowledged his great friend as the source of his understanding, as the source of existence itself. It was always Shams who led the way, who revealed the secrets, and who kept encouraging his young charge to open to the gaze. Shams urged him to continue gazing, even when Jalaluddin must have felt overwhelmed by the enormity of what he was entering into and frustrated by his inability to absorb everything that Shams was pouring into him.

And so Jalaluddin records this conversation:

> I said to him, "Your zeal is great,
> But your eyes look so small and slanted.
> If you know the secret, just come out with it
>   and tell me!"
>
> "My eyes are not small," he replied,
> "But the road to the secret is indeed narrow.
> Just keep looking at my narcissus eyes,
> And try to find a road from them to that which
>   you seek."

Shams may have been a feral human, a kind of wild child who so embraced the raw energies of his nature that he left behind the conventions of the civilized world into which he had been born, but he was also highly educated. It's quite likely that, in addition to his knowledge of Islamic teachings, he was conversant with the spiritual histories and traditions of other cultures as well. How illuminating that, of all the glorious flowers in God's garden that he might name to describe the beauty that drew Jalaluddin to his eyes, he would cite the narcissus; for its mythological history is so tied up with the practice of gazing.

In Greek mythology, Narcissus had been a youth of great beauty who had not returned the love of the goddess Echo, and his indifference to her longing had caused her to die of a broken heart. As punishment, he was forced to sit and gaze upon his own reflection in the clear waters of a spring and, like Echo, pined away inconsolably over his inability to consummate the intense longing and love that he felt toward the face that looked back at him. Finally, he was turned into the flower that we know today as a narcissus.

As a teacher, Shams knew that it wasn't possible to share the secret that he possessed through the medium of words. The only way to understand was to dive headfirst into the mystery itself, to do the practice, to continue doing the practice, to have the experience that the practice bestowed; only through that direct experience could the secret that couldn't be spoken be understood. And so he kept telling Jalaluddin that, in order to know and understand the great secret, he must keep looking at Shams's eyes, and then look some more.

For months they stayed secluded. Food was brought to them, but they ate very little. They feasted instead on the nourishment that the practice bestows.

Once the contact through the gaze is established, both participants can just surrender to the current that can be felt inevitably to animate the waters of the encounter. The movement forward then becomes effortless as every cell of the body, like every leaf in a freely flowing stream, is given over to this mighty, palpable power. In the twentieth century, the great Burmese meditation teacher U Ba Khin would call this current *nibbana dhatu*, the force of enlightenment that wants to become activated in the body and sweep clean the floors, walls, and ceilings of body and mind. If we can activate that force, then all the impurities of the body and mind will eventually be removed. The body then becomes an open conduit through which the energy of the Divine can pass with no impediment or distortion.

When the two great friends finally emerged from their retreat, they did so as open vessels, channels for the Divine. Radiant, in a state of ecstatic intoxication well known to the Sufi tradition, Jalaluddin spoke of them both as being one soul in two bodies. This phrase was not just a poetic image but also an accurate description of fact. As the Indian poet Kabir, a spiritual descendent of Jalaluddin's for whom the eye center was also of paramount importance, would say many centuries later:

> The soul in essence is one.
> Many are the bodies
> In which it takes abode.

Much to his bewilderment, Jalaluddin soon discovered that his students weren't nearly so thrilled about the transformation that had occurred in him as Jalaluddin was himself. He wanted them to see that what he was experiencing was the consummation of everything that he had been speaking about. It was no longer just words and dreams of far-off possibilities; in him and Shams the words had been made into flesh and spirit. All that his students could see, however, was that their young and revered master had come under the spell of this wild and unkempt creature, and they feared that they might lose him forever. Jalaluddin wanted them to revere and love Shams as he had come to, but Shams became the butt of ridicule and the object of jealousy instead.

It should be remembered that the relationship between Jalaluddin and Shams must have indeed appeared strange. No one knew what had been going on behind the closed doors of their retreat room. No one knew the exact nature of the practices that the two friends had been exploring. All that anyone knew was that their teacher was not the same anymore. Where before he had been disciplined and precise, the image of propriety and a perfect mouthpiece for the traditional teachings of Islam, now he had come under the spell of a purported madman. His sobriety and precision, along with his interest in scholastic discourse, had disappeared like clouds in an evening breeze.

Nor did Shams help matters much. True to his self, he returned the barbs of ridicule with barbs of his own and managed, in a short time, to alienate most of the elders as well as many of the younger students. It was one thing to gaze at Shams with total openness and adoration as Jalaluddin had been doing for several months, to penetrate past the surface of his face and eyes and journey deep into his soul; it was quite another to look at the outer package with its ragged clothing and disregard for convention.

A recurrent theme that would appear many years later in Jalaluddin's poetry, but which must have been initiated by his students' blindness to Shams's glory, was the difference between seeing with the eyes of the body and the eyes of the soul. The eyes of the body can see only the surface appearance of bodies, but the eyes of the soul see souls. They look into and through the eyes of others, for there they find the secret doorway that allows them to gain entrance into the soul:

> *The eye of the sea is one thing,*
> *The eye of the foam another.*
> *Leave the foam aside.*
> *See with the eye of the sea.*

Why content yourself with reflections on the surface when your eyes are perfectly capable of diving deep into the soul of the friend you're with? And when you soften your gaze and see deep into the soul of your partner, a wonderful miracle begins to occur: you begin to travel across the deep expanse of inner space and see directly into your own soul as well. And remember, your eyes are perfectly good. You just have to be willing to open them and look.

The students and elders of Konya, however, were unwilling to open their eyes to Shams. The situation continued to deteriorate until one day Shams did what had always come most naturally to him when he could no longer endure the blindness and pettiness around him: he left Konya to move along to the next station on his path. There were no good-byes to Jalaluddin, no explanations for what must have been obvious anyway. Shams simply left, and the devastating shock of the sudden departure of the one whom Jalaluddin had come to see and revere as the source of his own awakening was like an earthquake inside his soul and sent him tumbling into a pit of grief and despair. The glue that had held his inner and outer worlds together was gone and, like all bereft lovers before and after him, he fell apart.

It was at this point in Jalaluddin's life that, out of the despair and emotional ruin into which he'd fallen, he spontaneously began to speak in the language of poetry. Perhaps it began in the letters that he wrote to Shams, sending them off to all corners of the Islamic world, hoping beyond hope that one of them would reach their target, that Shams would receive it, realize how his absence was devastating Jalaluddin, and deign to return. Here's one of his early letters:

> *Know that with your departure my mind and*
> *faith have been stripped.*
> *This poor heart of mine no longer has patience*
> *or resolve.*
> *Don't ask me about my wan face, my troubled*
> *heart, or the burning in my soul.*
> *Come see with your own eyes, for no power of*
> *words can explain these things!*
> *My face turns brown like a loaf baked in your*
> *heat.*
> *Now I crumble like stale bread and am*
> *scattered.*

Over time, the letters to Shams would evolve into poems to the world. Jalaluddin knew that the letters were almost certainly not reaching Shams. Even if they were, he had no idea whether Shams would ever read them, let alone respond to them. But still he had to write them, as if the writing relieved a bit of the building pressure on his soul, keeping him from exploding. Every poet has an intended audience to whom his or her words are directed; when you first come across the sheer volume of poetic words that Jalaluddin uttered in his life, and which his close disciples faithfully recorded, it can be helpful to remember that everything he ever wrote can rightly be read as a letter to Shams.

> O my Beauty, I have fallen in Your love,
> I follow Your way.
> Your love is a sea, my heart looks like a fish.
> If you turn Your face from me,
> If I don't see You,
> My soul that resembles a fish will die.
> Fish cannot survive without water.
> It's the same for lovers, they cannot endure
> The separation from the Beloved
> Who took their hearts.

Have you ever loved in your life, loved so intensely and totally that the other became your sustenance, the fuel for your fire, fuel on which you became so completely dependent that you knew, if it were ever taken away, your light would simply go out, like a candle that has burned itself down with only a trail of wispy smoke remaining? Have you ever loved another so deeply and passionately that you truly came to believe in the notion of soul mates? Or have you ever joined another in a loving embrace where, from the bottom of your hearts, you both proclaimed your love for each other and acknowledged how you'd been searching for each other all your lives, only to wake the next morning to an empty bed, a note resting where your lover's body should be, a note telling you that things have somehow changed and that he or she doesn't want to play anymore? If you have, then you can perhaps understand Jalaluddin's devastation at losing Shams.

A year passed, a year of torment and isolation, and then word reached Jalaluddin that Shams had been seen in Damascus. Jalaluddin again poured out his pleading in a renewed round of letters, none of which were answered. Finally, he sent off his favored son, Sultan Veled, on the long journey to Damascus to find Shams and to entreat him to return to Konya. His son was able to find his father's friend and gave him assurances that the situation in Konya had changed, that through his father's despair people had finally come to understand who and what Shams was and that all had been forgiven. Shams agreed to return.

You can imagine the extraordinary joy that must have permeated the reunion of these two great friends as they bowed down to each other in the sands. Once again, they went into retreat and plunged anew into the practices that had ripped them open during their first immersion. These same practices now deepened and sustained the growth that had earlier occurred. During this retreat, Jalaluddin's understanding must have matured and ripened, and yet what was happening was still an incomprehensible mystery to him.

He so viewed Shams as the source of his awakening that he wasn't able to understand that the true source was the practice itself and that wherever two people join together and enter into each other's gaze the heart and soul come open. Only much later in life, after Shams had departed for good, was he able to understand this through entering into deep friendship with others. Then he knew that what had occurred between him and Shams was not just a function of Shams but was available to any two great friends who were willing to open to each other through the gaze and venture together into the depths of their shared soul. Much later he would write:

A saint went on a retreat to seek a sublime goal. A voice came to him, saying, "Such a sublime goal cannot be attained by means of solitary retreat. Leave your retreat so that you can encounter the gaze of a great man and, through that meeting, reach your goal."

But during his time with Shams, it was as though this ultimately gifted turner of phrases couldn't find the words to describe what was happening. In the deep embrace and union that the practice of gazing at the beloved so naturally leads to, it is certainly common enough not to be able to speak or even think. The experience of dissolving so far beyond the limits of what you ever conceived yourself to be can be so enormous and awe-inspiring that you can become dumbstruck by the sheer majesty of it all, incapable of making any conventional sense about what is occurring. This is one of those mysteries that cannot be solved; it can only be lived. And so Jalaluddin would write of this time with Shams:

> Both our sets of eyes became drunk,
> Utterly intoxicated by the promise of Union.
> O my God!
> What is this union of eye to eye?!

Remember that Jalaluddin was a scholar of Islam, a student of divine revelation as it was described through the traditional Islamic teachings, and suddenly here he found himself sitting face-to-face with the truth of that revelation, being drawn down into it like a stone sinking in water. A part of him must have wanted to stand aside, to sit on the bank of the river and observe what was occurring so that he could understand it with his mind and communicate it to others; and yet the larger part of him was swept away by currents that he could no longer resist.

Everything was so new to him. How could he describe it? How

could he share it with others? What should he even call it? And so, he asks:

> Now, what shall we call this new sort of gazing
>   house
> That has opened in our town
> Where people sit quietly and pour out their
>   glancing
> Like light, like answering?

There had been a long tradition in Sufism whereby the transmission of teachings would occur when the gaze of a teacher fell for a moment on the eyes of the student, but this was something entirely different. After hours and days and weeks of practice, it was no longer possible to tell who was student and who was teacher, who was the lover and who the beloved. And the holding of the gaze was not a brief and isolated event. Once the two friends had connected through the gaze, it was as if the ship of their souls had been launched, and the winds and currents just kept propelling it onward, ever farther, ever closer to its ultimate destination. This was not a one-way transmission. This was a mutual destruction of the limited, autocratic mind, as though a wrecking ball were bouncing back and forth between two buildings and demolishing both of them at the same time. The longer the gaze was held, the more thorough was the demolition of the limited sense of self that believes itself to be something other than God. The longer the two friends remained this way in visual contact, the more they kept on making space for the energies of the heart and the soul to pour through.

The two great friends emerged from their second retreat, and again the students could not fathom what Jalaluddin could possibly see in this mischief maker who kept luring their beloved teacher away from his family and duties. Where Jalaluddin beheld a diamond, the majority of his students could see only a darkened piece of coal, a rough and uncut gem at best. But to the rusted lock, the most homely key, if it fits, becomes breathtakingly beautiful.

Didn't his students know the story of Majnun and his love for Leyla? His love for and devotion to her were so complete that he couldn't even bear to look at another woman. Majnun's friends and family tried to direct him to consider many of the other truly beautiful women of the tribe, to break his single-minded obsession with this common woman whose looks were uninspiring compared to the beauty of these others. But Majnun couldn't be swayed. Leyla was the key that fit and opened his lock, and so Leyla was the only woman for whom he had eyes.

Jealousy is the most valueless of all human emotions, a refusal to accept and see the truth as it is, and it can breed horrific acts. No one knows for sure what happened, but one evening Shams was summoned from his room and never seen again. Most scholars believe that he was set upon and murdered, and quite possibly by Jalaluddin's other son, Aladdin Chelebi, who must have feared that the family enterprise, the legacy to which he felt entitled, was being threatened by the influence of this troublemaker.

Once again Jalaluddin fell into great despair, but this round of grief was somehow different from the first one, and over time it subsided with the growing acceptance and understanding that Shams's work had been completed. The perfect seed had taken root in the fertile soil of the perfect heart, and Jalaluddin grew to realize that Shams could never be taken from him. How could one ever be separated from one's own self? Bodies are separate and always will be, but the true soul, the heart of hearts, can only be one.

And so, for the rest of his life, he did the only thing that he could do. He sang and he danced, and every step and movement of his dance was a eulogy in flesh and motion to Shams, and every word of his poems was a shout of praise to his great departed friend. His dance lives on in the Mevlevi order that his son Sultan Veled founded after Jalaluddin's death, and his words cry out to us as loudly today as they did when they were first uttered to find a beloved friend, to take up the path of the heart, and to let the soul get ripped open by the glories that lie within, glories that are just waiting, sometimes patiently, sometimes not, to be released through the body and into the world.

The Two Worlds and the Lover's Resolution

The world in which we live is not the only world that exists. Inside the appearances of the world with which we're familiar, inside its sights, its sounds, its smells, sensations, and tastes lies a whole other dimension of experience, like a nutmeat inside a shell. An understanding of the differences between these two worlds can be of enormous help as we enter into the practice of gazing at the beloved, for the practice demands that we familiarize ourselves with the conditions peculiar to each world and learn how to move freely back and forth between the two. Not surprisingly, one of the most common, recurring themes to be found in Rumi's poetry is the existence of these two worlds—and the way in which their differences can ultimately be transcended:

Behind this world opens an infinite universe.

What is this universe, this other world, like? How does it differ from the world that most of us view as reality? Is it, in its way, as real as our familiar world? And, most important, if such a realm actually exists, and if entrance into this realm bestows real benefits and joys upon the traveler, how do we embark on this journey from the known into the unknown?

Questions abound, and the poet offers us visions as answers:

> *Everything you see has its roots in the unseen world.*
> *The forms may change, yet the essence remains*
>   *the same.*
> *Every wonderful sight will vanish, every sweet*
>   *word will fade,*
> *But do not be disheartened,*
> *The source they come from is eternal, growing,*
> *Branching out, giving new life and new joy.*
> *Why do you weep?*
> *The source is within you,*
> *And this whole world is springing up from it.*
> *The source is full,*
> *And its waters are ever-flowing.*
> *Do not grieve, drink your fill.*
> *Don't think it will ever run dry, this is the*
>   *endless ocean.*

An endless ocean and a finite world. Once again, more questions than answers present themselves. Which do you want for yourself? Which do you think is your true birthright as a child of God? And might it be possible to partake of both?

Most simply put, these two worlds are the world of separation and the world of union. When we look out upon the conventional world through the eyes of the body, all we see is separation, a multitude of unique and distinct objects, each one separate from the one sitting at its side, the window separate from the wall, the objects on the table separate from one another, the table separate from the floor, the bodies that walk across the floor separate from one another. In many ways we can take real pride in our ability to distinguish one object from its neighbor, for out of this discernment we've learned to survive, to differentiate berry from rock and water from earth.

The only problem with this way of seeing is that, by focusing exclusively on the distinctions between individual objects, we've lost sight of the common ground that binds all these objects together as a single whole that can never be severed—not by our hand, and not by any thought or strategy of perception. If we cling only to the vision of the world as a composite of distinct parts, each one a separate universe unto itself, existing through an uneasy truce with every other distinct part, then we become afraid and start to feel very lonely. We cut ourselves off from the rich and cohesive waters of which we are such an intimate part and become, instead, hardened and dry, a once fertile valley on which a drought has descended. From such a harsh and cold wilderness, all we can do is cry out for the source of comfort and wholeness that we may only dimly remember and feel.

We look at a tree and see it as separate from the earth in which it grows and the air that surrounds it; but how can the roots of the tree be separate from the soil that feeds it? How can we see the tree as separate from the sun and rain that allow it to grow? How can we separate ourselves from the life-giving oxygen that the tree releases into our lungs with every breath we take? If the birds that we love didn't have the branches of the tree for their home, where would they go? And aren't its berries and fruits a part of our flesh sitting patiently on the shelves of Earth's pantry, just waiting for their moment of transformation when we will pick and eat them and they will turn into movements in our bodies, thoughts in our minds, or the play of love between a man and a woman that will bring about the birth of a child?

When we look out upon the world in which we live through the eyes of the soul, however, a whole different vista springs suddenly into view. Objects may be many, but the soul is one, and so what the eyes of the soul see is the common ground of being that binds everything into one piece and process, the tree and the soil and the rain and the whole cycle of life. The primary purpose of spiritual practices, according to *A Course in Miracles,* is "to heal the separation," to help us recover from the nightmare of fear, alienation, and loneliness that separation breeds, and to reveal the profoundly interconnected and unified nature of the world of the soul.

When we sit with our great friend, pouring our gaze into the eyes of the beloved other and receiving his or her gaze in return, the world of separation disappears before our eyes, and together we merge back into a shared experience of union. We become one with our friend, and the nightmare of fear is replaced by the gentle dream—no, the reality—of love. Rumi describes the power we have to help each other heal our sense of separation:

> A corporeal being has such power that love for it can put a man into a state wherein he does not consider himself as separate from that being: all his senses, seeing, hearing, smell, and so forth become so absorbed in that corporeal being that no part of his body or soul desires anything else.

Where is the doorway that leads from separation to union to be found? Well, one of the ports of entry is through the narrow clefts of your beloved's eyes, for as you gaze at your great friend, as you pour yourself through that opening, something begins to happen to you both, and you no longer experience yourselves as separate from each other. The key turns in the lock, and a door springs open to reveal a world of experience that both looks and feels radically different from the familiar world on the other side. You actually feel that the core out of which both your individual bodies emerge is one and the same place. When two beings are able to meet in this way, soul-to-soul, their sense of separate self simply dissolves and is replaced by a penetrating and shared awareness of this fundamental unity as the real, lived experience of their individual bodies.

This is not just a fanciful and ethereal notion, devoid of substance and feeling. This place of union is as palpable as anything you can know and touch in this world. It is the birthright of your body and soul, as mystics everywhere have proclaimed. Mystics are often dismissed as dreamers within the scientific bias of our culture, but the best and brightest of them are skilled technicians of the soul, speaking to us with great precision of the palpable realities of the world of union.

For Rumi, true friendship sets into motion the alchemical transformation that occurs when two people are willing to open so deeply to each other that any awareness of separation between them is burned away like the driest kindling in a divine fire. Anything less than this alchemical transformation from separation into union is not real friendship. Any meeting that allows the two participants to maintain their illusion of separation is not a true meeting. As Rumi put it:

I would rather see my friends and gaze upon them to my fill—and they upon me—because when friends here in this life and world have seen each other's substance thoroughly, their friendship will gain in intensity as they enter into the other world.

Traditionally, the world of union has been viewed as the privileged vision of ascetic seekers, the spiritual practitioners who have given up interest in the sensory pleasures of the world of appearances and have focused all of their attention on the unseen reality that lies, so to speak, behind the scenes, just behind and underneath the scaffolding of creation. However, the path of the ascetic has always been crafted through denials and renunciations, and a tragic consequence of this stance has been a denigration of the lived experience and impulses of the human body and, by extension, the whole realm of the visible world. The body, with its joys and its sorrows, with its lusts and aversions toward other objects and bodies, can be viewed by ascetics as the obstacle that bars their passage from this world to the next, and so they forego intimate contact with others. The whole visible tableau of the world of nature—the stars, the land and water, the plants and animals and other human bodies—can be seen as a veil that keeps the vision of the other world concealed; through the enforced withdrawal of interest in this world the ascetic slashes away at that veil, trying to tear it down so that what it conceals may be revealed. The price the ascetic pays for this revelation is loneliness.

Rumi and Shams, however, tell us that there is a different way, a whole different approach to the world of union, one that doesn't force us to turn away in fear and loathing from the feeling body and the visible world. After all, if the experience of union is the true sanctuary of God, how could we ever think that we could enter into that inner sanctum through treating the world of God's creation as something tawdry or in need of transcending, a concealing curtain rather than the very show we have come to see? It just doesn't make sense.

This world in which we live does not need to be transcended for the experiential realm of union to appear. It needs, instead, to be fully entered into with no holding back. The visible world of reality is not an obstacle that bars our entrance into the realm of union. It is, instead, the very door that grants entrance into that realm:

> *Infinite mercy flows continually*
> *But you're asleep and can't see it.*
> *The sleeper's robe goes on drinking river water*
> *While he frantically hunts mirages in dreams*

And runs continually here and there shouting,
"There'll be water further on, I know!"
It's this false thinking that blocks him
From the path that leads to himself.
By always saying, "Further on!"
He's become estranged from "here":
Because of a false fantasy
He's driven from reality.

The notion that the doorway to union is somehow far away from where we sit or stand right now is a false fantasy. The building blocks of the reality of this moment and this world—the sights, the sounds, the sensations, the smells, the tastes, and even the thoughts about it all—are themselves the doorway through which we must pass if we wish to leave the world of separation behind and enter into the domain of union.

Whether we experience these building blocks as a veil that hides the other world or as the direct doorway to that world depends entirely on our state of mind and on the degree of relaxation and acceptance we experience in the body. This is where the true value of spiritual exercises comes into play. A mind that is lost in unconscious thought and a body that is tense and numb, unaware of the rich web of sensations of which it's spun, together act as an iron door that bars our entrance into this other dimension. But the same sensory phenomena, rightly relaxed into and perceived, open the crack between the two worlds, allowing the person to slip right through.

This mysterious doorway was here all the time, literally right in front of our eyes and under our noses! We'd just been looking all this time in the wrong direction, "looking for love," as the country song tells us, "in all the wrong places." To journey from the world of separation to the world of union, the cow doesn't jump over the moon but passes instead right through it.

Shams viewed the displays of piety of so many of his Sufi contemporaries as only shadows of real practice. For him, the practices of the time had become increasingly specious and suspect, long on fancy words and visions but short on real mystical substance. For him, reality itself was the one substantial door that must be acknowledged, experienced with all the senses, and passed through. Only through complete acceptance of the reality of this world can the greater reality of the other world be known. Fantasy can only lead us astray. Like a shepherd listening for the bells of his lost flock, we imagine sounds where there aren't any, and set off up the mountain in pursuit of these fictive signals.

One of the recorded stories tells of a visit Shams made to a well-known sheikh in Baghdad. When he arrived at the sheikh's residence, he found him gazing into a bowl filled with water. Shams inquired about the practice, and the sheikh is reported to have replied, "I am watching the moon in this basin." Behavior such as this always made Shams crazy, and he is reported to have cried out in frustration, "Unless you have a boil on the back of your neck, lift up your head and look at the sky! There you'll see the moon as it is, not in this basin. Why are you leaning over basins when all you're really doing is depriving yourself of what you're really looking for?"

Reality itself, whatever we can experience right now in this very moment, needs to be the object of our attention. We need, however, to look upon this world of appearances not just with the eyes of the body. We need to perceive the sounds, sights, and sensations through the eyes of the soul. The components of these two worlds are identical, composed as they both are of the sensory building blocks of reality. It's just that the world of union comes into clear focus through a softer and more relaxed perception of these building blocks. One could even say that, when we're lodged in our mind with its fearful tendencies to divide the fabric of reality into separate and discrete stitches, we see through the eyes of the body. But when we open to the feeling dimensions of our heart and to the love that draws us into communion with that which we gaze upon and interact with, then, and only then, do the eyes of our soul become activated.

Over and over again, Rumi urges us to differentiate between these two worlds, these two ways of seeing, these two very different paths, and these two ways of being, and then he exhorts us to make the right choice. Do we want to follow the way of the mind down through its endless maze of analysis and dissection, or do we want to enter into the way of the heart? The heart can accomplish what all the king's horses and men, with all their great strength and intellect, were unable to do for the hapless Humpty Dumpty—it can put all the pieces back together again. In the words of Rumi:

> *The way of the mind is discussion, inquiry,*
> *Wagering, obstinacy, objection,*
> *Approval and disapproval.*
>
> *The way of the heart is pleasure,*
> *Ecstasy, honey, and sugar.*

If the person who sees only with the eyes of the body misses the beauty and grace of the other world, so does the ascetic miss out on the joys that can come only from engaging fully with life, from living out one's humanity rather than running from it under the pretext of spiritual endeavor. Ultimately, the two worlds can be experienced as blending into one, and each can be perceived as completing the other rather than being in conflict with it. If such a blended vision is not possible for either the ascetic or the worldly wise, who, then, can gain access to this understanding?

Rumi is very explicit in his answer, and it is one of the greatest of all the gifts that the Sufi path has bestowed on us. An understanding that's able to view the worlds of separation and union simultaneously, to resolve their apparent conflict, and to go beyond the limits inherent in each one is available only to lovers:

> There is no solution for the soul but to fall in
>   love.
> It has to creep and crawl amongst the lovers first.
> Only lovers can escape from these two worlds.
> This was written in creation.
> Only from the heart can you reach the sky.
> The rose of glory can only be raised in the heart.

Over and over again, Rumi pleads with us, if we want to know God, to become a lover!

> Wherever you are, in whatever circumstances
>   you may be, strive to be a lover.

He even tells us:

> The way you make love is the way
> God will be with you.

Lovers live fully in this world. They need not run away from it. And yet, through pouring their love (what else can they do?) into the soul and body of their beloved, they pass through the veil that ordinarily keeps the two worlds separate. Thus, they partake of the richness of both. True lovers become so mixed together that it becomes difficult to differentiate the two. Like droplets of mercury that have fallen on a wooden floor, they possess an inner magnetism that draws them back together where, once joined, it becomes difficult for them ever again to become separate in their souls:

> *At breakfast, a lover asked her lover, as a test:*
> *"Whom do you love more? Me or yourself?"*
> *He replied, "I'm so annihilated in you,*
> *I'm filled with you from head to foot.*
> *Nothing's left of my own life but my name:*
> *The rest is you. I'm dissolved like vinegar*
> *In your ocean of burning honey,*
> *I'm like a stone transformed into a ruby,*
> *I've been filled with the sun's glory."*

While the physical bodies of lovers must always remain separate, their souls are joined together in union, and through this dual awareness they transcend the differences between the two worlds. Such an awareness parallels another famous saying from both the Christian and Sufi traditions, which is given as advice on how to live in this world even when we know of the other world's existence: "Live in this world, but not of it." In other words, make your way through life with the fullest awareness of the sounds, the sights, the smells and sensations in which you swim, but always stay mindful of the pearls that lie inside these outer shells. Don't just content yourself with the messages that come off their surfaces. Dive deeply right into and through them and enjoy the deep secret that they hold inside. Don't just content yourself with the visible world or its unseen shadow, one without the other. Instead, juggle both so rapidly and skillfully in your hands that they begin to blur together and merge. And the easiest and most direct way to become one of God's chosen jugglers is to fall in love and become a lover.

It feels important at this point to clarify the nature of love that Rumi is referring to here. Ordinarily, when we think of lovers, we think of two people who are so drawn to each other that they entwine their bodies together in the sacred act of making physical love. This urgency to come together in procreative play is as deep and beautiful an impulse as exists in our bodies. However, when we fall into love through encountering the gaze of a great friend, something entirely different may begin to occur between us. It's not just body that copulates with body, but soul that copulates with soul, and through the divine intercourse that transpires, the two lovers impregnate each other and give birth, not to a child, but to the great ground of being itself. They allow this great ground to use their bodies as a conduit through which it can manifest itself here on Earth.

It may be that great friends who enter into the practice of gazing at the beloved together will find that they're drawn to become physical lovers as well (later in this book we will address this possibility), but it needs to be stressed that the extraordinary merging and profound realization of love that the practice naturally spawns may occur without one body ever physically touching the other. The practice is not one in which, necessarily, physical bodies make love, but one in which souls go out of their minds with the passion of their lovemaking.

In physical lovemaking, there is always the possibility that we'll remain separate from our lover, that our bodies and fluids will join together and intermingle, but that our minds and souls will remain aloof, observing it all from a safe distance. In the practice of gazing at the beloved, our bodies may remain separate and at a distance, but our souls, the very essence of our beings, will not only penetrate each other but become one with the other. This is how deep and complete the merging in this kind of play naturally becomes. To make physical love, we need to give up our inhibitions and join our body with our lover's body. To make the love of souls that Rumi is telling us about, we need to give up our mind, our belief in our existence as separate beings, and join our soul with our lover's soul. The act of gazing at the beloved can become breathtakingly intimate as, together, we venture back to the one soul, our common ground of being that, once it appears, truly shatters our ability to pretend any longer that our sense of separate self describes the whole of what we are. And as wonderful and intimate as physical lovemaking can be, it can also all too often be used as a defense against falling into this deepest of intimacies.

Without an understanding of the practice of gazing at the beloved, the relationship between Jalaluddin and Shams looks very perplexing indeed. Without this understanding, it's easy to see how some interpreters have concluded that they must have been physical lovers, for how else could they have opened to such ecstasies of love and merging as they routinely reported? And certainly the very real possibility of their being physical lovers must have been one of the issues that disturbed Jalaluddin's students and followers, as homophobia and intolerance toward same-sex lovers are not new inventions of our age. Personally, I think it unlikely that they were physical lovers, but I would also hasten to add that it matters not a bit whether they were or not. The large love between them was spawned by rubbing their souls together through the deep penetration of their mutual gaze, and there are times in the practice when it actually feels as though the energies of one heart and soul are rhythmically moving in and out of the other. What Jalaluddin and Shams were each opening to through the other was a love greater than love.

Become a lover. This is Rumi's message to us. Meet another at the very depths of your being. Let your soul penetrate your lover's soul. Bodies alone cannot bring the soul back to itself. Don't be satisfied with the body's imitation of the reunion into the great ground of being that you so long for. If it's a physical love that you have with your great friend, then rejoice and enjoy and love your lover with every cell and thrust of your body, but never forget the deeper copulation that you both seek, whose climax is the only human experience that can produce the contentment that your soul craves.

Never shy away from the pull of love. Rumi, and all the Sufis, are so clear about this. Always risk love when you feel it calling you, strumming the tissues of your being like a musician caressing the strings of a lute. God wants you to love because you and God are one, and only by becoming a lover do you stand the best chance of remembering this most shattering of truths. Yes, the path of love is strewn with unforeseen challenges and heartaches and soul mines, but even these, as we will see later, are part of the path as well. They have their place, and they have their purposes. If we avoid love's thorns, we never ever smell the fragrance of its flowers. If we avoid love's pains, we never ever taste its privileged pleasures. So never run from love. To run from love is to run from yourself, and that is a race you can never win.

Find your friend, take up the practice together, and begin your journey back to the home to which you so long to return. Whatever you do, trust love, even if it turns your life upside down:

> *May anyone who says, "Save him from love!"*
> *Have his prayer chased from heaven!*

The practice of gazing at the beloved is like a prayer to heaven, a call to love, and its cries are always answered. A vehicle (part automobile, part boat) suddenly arrives at your front door, and you and your beloved friend are escorted away from the flat and dry land of separation into the life-giving waters of union. Gazing at your friend summons the great ground of being to make its presence felt, and it begins to tug at you, asking you to come back home to your soul's birthplace.

3

Body of Separation, Body of Union

*M*any of our traditional religions and spiritual paths unwittingly contribute to the very separation that they seek to heal by their insistence on splitting the human being into two distinct parts, a body and a soul, and by then elevating the value of the soul while simultaneously denigrating the value of the body. These traditions teach us that the body is the problem; that it is to be viewed with suspicion and disdain; that the body (and, by extension, the whole world of appearances) must be transcended in order to find God; that the body is like a fence of barbed wire that the soul must leap over in order to free itself from its imprisonment.

In the practice of gazing at the beloved, however, just the opposite is true. The body is the path itself, the doorway through which we must pass, the chamber into which we must enter if we wish to reclaim our birthright and connect back to our soul. Or, as Rumi tells us:

Although the light of soul is essential,
Nobody has reached that sky without a body.

The problem is not with the body. The problem is that we have created an erroneous belief that all we are is the body. In the world of separation, we identify ourselves very narrowly with our physical visible body to the exclusion of everything and everyone else: the space and objects surrounding us, the distant stars, other bodies. The most direct result of this belief is an implosion of identity that splits the world irrevocably into two. Everything inside the container of my physical body is exclusively "me," and everything that I can perceive to exist outside this container is "other than me." I want to repeat again: the body is not the problem. The profound sense of separation and alienation that is the natural consequence of this split is the problem.

By embracing this belief, we effectively trade away our shared participation in the soul's domain, the great ground of being, for exclusive, proprietary ownership over this one small parcel of real estate, our physical body. The result of this trade is for each of us to become an "I," separate and distinct from everything else. We forfeit the world of union and take up permanent residence in the land of separation. We then create a highly sophisticated pattern of tension in our body, much like the placing of a colored filter over a camera shutter, so that our experience of reality appears to conform to this erroneous belief. The result, not surprisingly, is a buildup of physical and emotional pains and pressures and, if we're honest with ourselves, a pervasive sense of bewilderment and fear.

Paradoxically, the way that we can free ourselves from this limiting belief that all we are is the body, separate from everything that we can perceive to exist outside its borders and boundaries, is by completely surrendering into and embracing the lived experience of the body itself. When we allow ourselves to relax into our physical presence in this very moment and actually experience what the body feels like, we realize that this belief does not accurately reflect the reality of that experience.

The lived experience of the body can be known only through an awareness of the minute, shimmering sensations that can be felt to exist in every one of its parts down to the smallest cell. Sometimes, you can feel these sensations like a subtle tingling or electrical current passing through you. Other times, they may gather together into a compacted ache or a generalized feeling of dullness. They may feel like soft falling rain one moment only to turn into the most malevolent thunderstorm the next, and then a tropical sun may peek out from behind the clouds and dry everything out. Sometimes, they may feel like chorus lines of millions upon millions of DNA strands dancing with abandon, wave after wave, across the stage of your body, light as air, the tiny tips of their shoes barely grazing your skin. Other times, they can be like legions of storm troopers throwing themselves into battle as strong surges of feeling erupt through your body with passionate intensity. These sensations are constantly changing their form and feeling from moment to moment, billowing and subsiding, ebbing and flowing, shape-shifting in a never ending parade of tactile throbs, quivers, tingles, and palpitations, all the time marching to the decidedly organic beat of their own internal drummer.

Ordinarily, however, we're aware of only a tiny fraction of the sum total of the body's tactile sensations. We block our awareness of them through the exact same pattern of tension and resistance that creates the distorting lens that allows the perspective of separation to come into focus. Even though we may philosophically believe that all we are is our body, we don't give ourselves permission truly to experience what the body actually is. The body then becomes a concept in our minds, a pale object held at arm's length, a something that we distantly have rather than the lived experience of what we immediately are in this very moment. If we can begin to relax our resistance and bodily tensions, however, our sensations begin to reappear, and the distorting lens falls from our eyes.

Rumi was well aware of the tragic consequences of the devaluation of the body in favor of the rarefied maneuverings of the mind that, divorced from a felt awareness of bodily presence, can get so quickly and literally out of touch with the grounded, lived mystery of existence. Untethered to the experience of the body as a unified field of tactile sensations, the mind can all too easily float away like a hot-air balloon that has neither ballast to stabilize itself nor pilot at the helm.

Rumi's father, Bahauddin Veled, had himself been a mystic and spiritual seeker of considerable stature who recorded his insights in a book that he then passed along to his son. In contrast to the prevailing dismissal of the spiritual value of the body, he wrote frankly and passionately about the principle of *ma'iyya*, the recognition that the presence of God needs to be experienced not just in the heart, not just in the mind, but as a feeling in every small part and cell of the body.

Only through kindling an awareness of the whole body as a unified field of tactile sensations can we become whole, move beyond our fearful and claustrophobic belief in our isolation and separation, and enter again into the soul's embrace in the domain of union. One of the great tragedies of human life is that we have been subtly influenced by our culture to block out and squash the awareness of our body by resisting the currents and flows of the sensations that can be felt to animate it. And then we wonder why our soul remains so elusive, apparently in hiding, unwilling to show its face.

The reason that we need to stress the importance of reembracing the experience of the body as a critical component in the reclamation of our soul is that the practice of gazing at the beloved greatly magnifies our awareness of the tactile sensations of the body. Without this understanding, the initial contact that occurs between us and our great friend may feel very unusually intense and perplexing indeed. As we sit and gaze at our beloved friend, we begin to feel our bodily sensations much more strongly than we ordinarily do, like ghosts that come out of hiding on All Hallows' Eve. Where formerly we may not have been able to feel much at all, suddenly we're flooded with tactile sensations that sweep through us like strong currents and tidal flows:

> *The most important dance is the one that*
> *   happens inside us.*
> *Particles of our body are dancing*
> *With hundreds of different rhythms and grace.*

To the degree that we can accept these strong waves of sensation, yielding completely to their organic impulses and movements, we stay connected to our friend and keep moving, like a leaf in a swiftly flowing stream, toward our ultimate shared destination in the world of union. The surges of feeling-presence that erupt in the body can be extraordinarily powerful. In the deepest throes of the gazing embrace with our friend, the sensations may so fill and consume us that we directly experience the foolishness of creating concepts like *body* and *soul* and then crafting distinctions between them. The body becomes filled with light through the radiant effulgence of its sensations and loses its sense of solidity and heaviness. Simultaneously, we can feel the emerging presence, replete with feelings, of what we can only call soul. The merging of these two formerly distinct concepts into one lived experience caused Rumi to utter, in the midst of the deep, palpable intermingling of his soul with the soul of Shams:

> *I have no idea whether I am a bright soul*
> *or a bright body.*

Just as we are unconscious of the full and rich range of sensations that fill our body from head to foot, so too are we unaware that at this very moment we're sitting at the place that's been set for us at the table of union. Union isn't a condition that we need heroically to create and build from scratch. We don't need to mill its wood and assemble its pieces. It's here right now, free for the taking, but we need to wake up to that fact and take it.

If we remain unaware of our bodily presence, searching perhaps for the soul in the isolated pantry of our mind, we'll very likely find the shelves bare and remain hungry and unfulfilled. Famished, we walk through a dense orchard in which the ripest and most delicious fruits hang heavily from every branch of every tree, but in our exhaustion our head droops, our gaze falls to the ground, and we pass through the orchard as though it didn't exist. If we kindle the awareness of our body as a unified field of sensations, however, the world of union is revealed as having existed right in front of our eyes all the time, and we can eat to the content of both stomach and heart. In the aftermath of filling ourselves with the object of our heart's longing, we glow brightly, both as soul and as body.

Rumi exhorts us not to make the all too common spiritual mistake of viewing the body as a somehow unworthy companion on the journey to the land of union, relegating it to the untidy garbage heap of things we may believe we need to leave behind if we are truly to get on with the real task at hand. For Rumi, kindling an awareness of the indwelling presence that bursts forth and blossoms through the body is the real task at hand, and so he reminds us:

> Inside your body is a priceless treasure,
> A gift from the eternally generous One.
> Look for that gift inside of you.

The whole object of our search is this priceless gift that lives inside us, inside our body, and our task is to find it, to take it out of storage, and to start wearing it again as the garment that most reflects our true nature.

Have you ever been given a simple article of clothing that so embarrassed you that you hid it away at the bottom of a dresser drawer, only to find it many months or years later, at which point you want to wear it all the time? The natural, simple sensations of the body are very much like that article of clothing. Our culture encourages all of us to feel ashamed of our normal bodily sensations. If we had no shame, we would feel our bodies in their totality without doubting the "rightness" of our physical experience. We would surrender with complete trust to that feeling-presence, acknowledging it as the one infallible guide capable of leading us back to the land of union.

It is inside our body, Rumi tells us, that the priceless gift of union is to be found. Inside our body we encounter the current of the life force, the animating power behind our sensations and behind consciousness itself. The sensations of the body are the first signs of the land of union, just as the new green buds on the trees are the first signal of the arrival of spring. Once we learn how to kindle an awareness of bodily sensations, we realize that the full energy of the life force wants to burst forth through our body just as it moves through a tree in springtime, causing the branches to explode with fresh buds. We've held them in and contained them for so long. We've resisted the arrival of spring, but as we learn to reembrace the sensations of our body, yielding to the current that can be felt to propel those sensations, the current that wants to move through us like freely flowing water, our soul bursts into bloom.

Through fearfully resisting the freest and fullest expression of the current of the life force as it manifests through the sensations of the body, we are tragically missing having a love as large as the universe itself explode through our body and mind until no trace of us (with our concerns, our worries, our unfulfilled hopes, our dissatisfactions) remains and we become that love. What we're actually bracing ourselves against out of fear and shame—sad irony—is love itself.

We're like millionaires who have taken to begging for small change on the street, hoping to collect enough money for a modest meal when we could sit down at a banquet table any day of the week.

And, Rumi reminds us, don't think that the current of the life force that is everybody's inheritance resembles a barely trickling stream. It's more like the mighty ocean itself:

> *The body is a device to calculate*
> *The astronomy of the spirit.*
> *Look through that astrolabe*
> *And become oceanic.*

In the land of separation, the experience of the body lies neglected. Overlooked in this way, it becomes hardened, a rocky creek bed after a drought. The rekindling of awareness of our sensations (they were there, remember, all the time) is like a cloudburst that moistens the ground, causing vegetation to grow anew, waters to build again and flow along the creek beds, dissolving the hardened sandstone rocks that have formed in their absence, and eventually pouring themselves into the suddenly not so distant ocean.

All waters eventually reach the ocean. It's every bit as much their purpose and destiny as it is the purpose of the waters of the life force that flow through the creek bed of the body to become a mighty river leading to the ocean of union, sweeping the awareness of the bodily being right along with it.

When we gaze at our beloved friend for extended periods of time, we begin to have glimpses of the ocean in ourselves. We know the ocean through its greatness of depth, and we feel the depth of our own being. We know the ocean as an energy that needs to be respected, the giver of joy and the taker of life, and so we respect and honor the energies that move through us. We know the ocean as the unending sequence of waves that break upon the beach, and so we familiarize ourselves with the waves of sensation that slosh back and forth along the shoreline of our body.

We may start off like individual snowflakes, frozen and distinct, each one unique and different from its neighbor, but end up, all of us, like a powerful river flowing back to the ocean of union:

> *The snow says all the time:*
> *"I'll melt, become a torrent,*
> *I'll roll toward the sea,*
> *For I'm part of the ocean!"*

Through the practice of gazing at the beloved, the tactile sensations, the emotional feelings, the pulsations and tidal flows of bodily energy are kindled and brought to awareness. We then learn to accept and honor them exactly as they are without judgment, for once they've been accepted the process of surrender can spontaneously begin. Through the deeply organic process of surrender, we're ushered back to the source of being that is paradoxically both our destiny and our origin.

It's important to emphasize that the practice of gazing at the beloved does not manipulate our experience in some artificial way; rather it takes us through a completely natural process that teaches us to come out of resistance and yield to what's real. As we kindle an awareness of the feeling-presence of the body through holding the gaze of our friend, we discover that the sensations are animated by a kind of current, not unlike the force that moves water through a river, and we learn simply to surrender to this current. As we become more comfortable in the practice, we learn to trust again in the wisdom of this current and allow it to take us wherever it wants. In this way, we reconnect with the great river of life itself.

Sometimes the course of this river may be smooth and gentle. Other times, it may be almost unbearably rough. But it's always taking us back home, in the direction of the reclamation of our birthright, to an ultimate union with the many different faces of the energies of God and the Goddess, playing together at last.

Traditional spiritual practices that teach us to deny or transcend the body cut themselves off from the only source of energy capable of successfully fueling their search. Realizations occur, but they tend to take us into rarefied and ethereal realms that, lovely as they are, lack the primal energy of the great ground of being in which our soul resides. For temporary visions of the beauty of starry nights, we forfeit our full participation in the energies that actually fuel the stars and our planet and our bodies. Sensations, not thoughts, are the medium through which soul makes its presence felt.

The late Terence McKenna eloquently described the distinction between the two approaches to God—denying the body or entering fully into its experience—in this way:

> It's not, as Milton said,
> "The God who hung the stars like lamps in heaven,"
> but it's the god of the oceans,
> and the jungles,
> and the icecaps,
> and the rivers,
> and the glaciers,
> and the great schools of fish,
> and the deserts.
>
> It's the goddess of the earth.
> It's the mind of organic life on this planet.

Through the practice of gazing at the beloved, we let go of heroic struggle and the forcible attempt to become something other than what we are. Instead, we simply relax into our felt sense of presence and become who and what we are in this very moment, one with our nature. Traditional spiritual paths that pass judgment on the physical body and brand it as something that needs to be transcended inadvertently create a subtle undercurrent of self-hatred that is, in the end, inimical to the reclamation of love and wholeness that is the professed goal of those paths. Without fully realizing it, these teachings subtly support the most pervasive and crippling lie that we all entertain about ourselves: that who I am is not okay; that who I am is in need of improvement or fixing. The only attitude that can take us home is the attitude of love, and love is a function of acceptance, pure and simple.

The practice of gazing at the beloved teaches us that the indwelling presence that we seek is here right now, always has been here, and always will be here. We're not like a batch of bad apples with something fundamentally wrong at our core. Our job is not to fix anything about ourselves (if it ain't broke, don't fix it!), but simply to relax deeply into our felt sense of presence, however it appears right now. By accepting our sensations and feeling states exactly as they appear, the obstructions and residues that obscure our immaculate, bright core begin to fall away. Like a leaf in a stream, we're drawn back to our home.

What kind of religion, then, are we talking about here? Clearly, it's not a religion of lofty concepts that hover several inches above the ground, disconnected from the vital energies that once, long ago, must have informed the seminal visions out of which that religion was born. No, the religion that Rumi is showing us is a religion plugged directly into those energies—and where can we possibly experience those energies except through the body? Rumi was revered in his time not just by the Muslims of Konya, but by the Jews and the Christians as well, each of whom saw in Rumi the embodiment of the deepest truths of their own faiths. Individual beliefs are as numerable as leaves on a tree. By focusing on the denominator common to all these beliefs, the one great trunk of the tree, Rumi spoke to the hearts of all people, regardless of their faith.

What kind of religion are we talking about here? Rumi is perfectly clear about this and provides the answer:

> *The work of religion is nothing but astonishment;*
> *Not the kind that comes from turning your*
> *   back on God*
> *But the kind that comes from being wild with*
> *   ecstasy,*
> *From being drowned in God and drunk on the*
> *   Beloved.*

And, elsewhere, he elaborates on the drunkard who expresses his love so freely and passionately:

> *So he speaks, and everyone around him*
> *Begins to cry with him, laughing crazily,*
> *Moaning in the spreading union*
> *Of lover and beloved.*
> *This is the true religion. All others*
> *Are thrown-away bandages beside it.*

Let us never turn our back on God's creation, on the water and the mountains and the plants and the trees and the starry sky and on the physical body itself. It's no large wonder that Rumi became a dancer as a result of his explosive encounter with Shams. To be a true dancer, you must become intimately aware of your body, feeling every small part and all the ways it wants to move. When we hold any little part of the body still, we effectively dull our awareness of the body's sensations. When we surrender to the current of sensations that wants to race through us like water through a sluice, the body may spontaneously begin to move and to dance, for this is the natural way that it expresses real joy.

A dancer truly befriends his or her body, every little piece and parcel, leaving nothing out, not a single muscle fiber, not a single sensation, not a single movement; this is true friendship. Jalaluddin and Shams became best of friends, for in the other each found someone who could meet and receive him, someone who could accept him totally, someone to whom he could reveal all of himself, leaving nothing out. Then, through their friendship, they became best of friends with the indwelling presence that the practice connected them to.

They befriended the world of union and merged with it just as they had befriended each other and merged with each other. Together, hand in hand, eye-to-eye, they entered back into the garden of souls. Only now when they walked among the fruit trees there, they did so with their heads held high, in full cognizance and enjoyment of the fruits that hung so thickly from the branches.

The blessings of the practice of gazing at the beloved are like a deliciously ripe fruit hanging from the branches of a tree, waiting to be plucked. And there are a multitude of allies supporting you in your harvest. In truth, the fruit of the world of union wants you to take it and bite into it every bit as much as you may want to take and taste it for yourself. The fruit of the world of union is calling to you, summoning you at this very moment to come and reclaim it. Can you feel its pull as you read this? Are you courageous enough to take it fully into your mouth and taste it? Are you courageous enough to return to the land of your birthright?

> A sweet voice came
> From the threshold of greatness.
> "Come," it says to soul.
>
> How could soul stay?
> How could a fish out of water stand still
> With the sound of the waves

Coming from the calm sea to his ears?
The fish wants to jump in the water.

The power to seize this moment lies within you and is fueled by the dormant energies of your body, which are just waiting for that little nudge that will wake them from their nap. Once these energies are fully awakened, we naturally turn our gaze toward God, just as a flower in full bloom naturally turns to face the sun. Human beings have an extraordinary opportunity to embrace the world of union, for we've been made in the reflected image of God:

The body is a mirror of heaven;
Its energy makes angels jealous.

The perspectives on the body and on the worlds of separation and union that have been presented in this first section create both the foundation on which the practice of gazing at the beloved can be successfully and safely erected and the context that will make sense of the experiences that you are likely to encounter. Let us now turn directly to the practice itself.

PART II

Funnels into God

The unrelated human being lacks wholeness, for he can achieve wholeness only through the soul, and the soul cannot exist without its other side, which is always found in a "You." Wholeness is a combination of I and You, and these show themselves to be parts of a transcendent unity.

Carl Gustav Jung,
The Psychology of the Transference

I think there's a dimension of love that's far beyond what we know in terms of healing, in terms of expansion. You can experience the healing that's going on through the love that exists between two people; you can see the light in the other's body and you can feel it in your own. It's a huge energy.

Marion Woodman in *Conscious Femininity: Interviews with Marion Woodman*

4

Gazing at the Beloved

Some spiritual teachers stand on the rooftops of buildings, calling out to the people gathered below in the streets, proclaiming the glories and beauty of the vista that they've been privileged to behold. For those of us standing in the streets, the accounts of their visions can provide deep inspiration and awe, and yet we're left wondering, "How could we possibly scale those heights ourselves?" Other teachers say little about their own experiences, preferring instead to craft ladders that they then lower down to the people milling about, exhorting them to begin the climb and observe the glories with their own eyes.

Rumi does both. He sings of the most resplendent visions, regaling us through the magic of his words, painting pictures of what the world of union and the domain of the heart and soul look like as viewed from on high. And then he offers practical guidance on how to scale those heights for ourselves.

Of all the specific practices that he cites, none is more frequently mentioned than the practice of gazing at the beloved. References to the eyes and to the practice of gazing appear everywhere in his writings, and we will draw on these passages in the chapters that follow as commentary on different aspects of the practice. There is one passage, however, that must be shared right at the outset, for the whole of the practice is described and contained in its three pregnant lines, and we will keep referring back to it as our primary guide in the pages that lie ahead:

> *Friend sits by Friend,*
> *And the tablets appear.*
> *They read the mysteries off each other's*
> *forehead.*

To begin the practice, all that you need to do is to sit down somewhere with your great friend. In truth, the practice can be explored in any posture. You can stand with your friend. You can dance with your friend. You can lie down with your friend. In the beginning, however, the simplest way to enter into the practice is to sit across from your friend so that you can look directly at each other. It isn't necessary to sit in a formal meditation posture like a Buddha with your legs crossed underneath you, especially if this posture is uncomfortable for you. What is far more important is that you are both able to relax completely in each other's presence. Opposite ends of a large sofa with high, supporting arms and cushions make for ideal seats.

Simply sit down with your friend. Sit comfortably. Face each other. To the best of your ability, limit the distractions around you. Soft lighting and a minimizing of noise are both helpful. *Friend sits by Friend.* This position creates the crucible for the experiment that's about to begin, the beaker that can contain the mixing together of the two friends, one an "I," the other a "You." Once you're seated comfortably, directly across from each other, the stage is set for the practice to unfold. Rumi gives us the most important of all the ensuing instructions in one small sentence:

Look as long as you can at the friend you love.

Look at each other. Truly look at each other. Focus your gaze on the eyes of your friend while your friend focuses his or her gaze on yours. And then hold each other's gaze. Hold it as long as you can without looking away.

In most conventional social interactions, either at work or at play, we rarely look at the person to whom we're speaking. Our eyes, like the eyes of dreamers, dart here and there and only occasionally come to rest on the eyes of the one we're addressing. The practice of gazing at the beloved provides a potent remedy, calamine lotion for the soul, for the lack of connection that our cultural habits of interaction so successfully breed, like mosquitoes in a swamp.

Let yourself look directly into the eyes of your friend. In a passage that reads like a travel advertisement for the practice, Rumi entices us with these words:

> *Come to the sea of charm and beauty.*
> *Arrive at the mine of Union.*
> *Gaze into the drunken eyes of that real beauty.*

Where should you focus your eyes? Should you look at both eyes together or choose a single eye on which to rest your gaze? In truth, there are no fixed rules here other than that you should look at your friend, relax completely, and see where your gaze naturally falls. Oftentimes, you will find that your eyes are naturally drawn to focus on your friend's left eye. At other times, however, the impulses may shift, and you feel your gaze drawn to your friend's right eye. And at other times still, you may find yourself gazing into both eyes simultaneously. Let your own feelings in the moment determine where you focus your gaze, and then realize that over time that focus may change.

Dive into that sea which is full of glory.
Plunge into these languid eyes.

As soon as your eyes lock onto the eyes of your friend, you will both feel a subtle but unmistakable sensation in the middle of your head, just behind the eyes. This is the initial sign that the energies of one soul are beginning to commingle with the energies of another, joining forces to create the ferry that will usher you both all the way to the land of union. Just as copper wires need to be linked together before energy can flow through the completed circuit, so too do you and your friend need to link up if you wish to create a force powerful enough to dispel the misperception of separation.

Physical contact alone isn't capable of establishing this linkage. Only the mutual touch of souls is powerful enough for this purpose, and for this task we have our eyes and the power of vision. How can the eyes alone establish such a linkage? As Ida Rolf, one of the great somatic teachers of the twentieth century, explained: "Vision is touch at a distance." Even though there is physical distance between you and your friend, the energy of your soul projects itself along the trajectory of your gaze until it meets and touches the soul of your friend. Both of you can feel this.

Look at your friend while he or she looks at you. Touch him or her through your gaze, and let yourself be touched through your friend's. Look at your friend from that place in the middle of your head, just behind your eyes, where you most know yourself to exist, and focus your gaze so that it comes to rest on the same place in your friend's head. Sufis have spoken of this special place as "the clear bead at the center."

Ordinarily, this center spot is concealed and protected by the many masks, personae, and limiting identities that we wear, like gauze veils covering our face, as we move about in the world. To touch this place with your gaze, you may have to make your way gingerly, layer by layer, through these protective shields and masks in much the same way as a meteorological researcher must fly through the buffeting winds of a hurricane's outer shells before reaching the calm of the hurricane's eye. Feel your gaze as an arrow that is loosed from the bow of your soul and that passes through the layers of your friend's masks until it hits the mark, and then feel your friend's gaze piercing through your veils and curtains of personality until it comes to rest, a perfect shot, in the center of your being:

> *If there are hundreds of curtains*
> *In one eye, his arrow-shaped eyebrow*
> *Pierces them all at once.*

Once the arrows of your mutual gaze strike their targets, the door to the land of union begins to open. The sensation in your head starts to spread, and you'll begin feeling sensations cropping up elsewhere in your body where, a moment before, you felt nothing. Areas of the body may suddenly begin to tingle and buzz, as though honeybees were probing the flowers of your cells. The body may begin subtly to shimmer, as though reflections of light were skipping across its waters. A cloud layer lifts and the sun comes out, clearing away the cold and rain, drawing the minute sensations of the body out of hiding just as it draws out new grass in a freshly seeded lawn. You and your friend begin entering into a different world together.

For Rumi, Shams became the sun, the warming source of life that drew his soul out of its cold hiding place and around which he had no choice but to revolve, like a planet orbiting a star:

> *Every particle of my body*
> *Is in love with your sun.*
> *Look carefully.*

The merchants of particles have endless
business to transact with the sun.

The discrete minute sensations that you begin to feel in your body are like individual droplets of water in a mighty river. As you continue to hold the gaze of your great friend, ever more sensations will be activated and brought to awareness, and over time the entire body may transform itself into a freely flowing river of sensations passing right through you. The river may move gently and nourish you. It may move roughly and challenge you. It doesn't matter. Your task is simply to relax as fully as you possibly can into the unusual and magnified sensations and perceptions that the practice kindles; accept whatever occurs exactly as it appears; and then surrender to the current that can inevitably be felt to animate the waters of your experience. Let's examine each of these aspects of the practice individually.

Relaxation

Tension is like a shattered pane of glass. It blocks the clear perception of what lies behind it and even causes us not to want to look in the first place. Unnecessary tension is a curtain that keeps the sensations of the body well hidden. To bring the principle of ma'iyya fully into your practice (that principle of experiencing God in every cell of the body), you want to lift that curtain so that the great play of bodily sensations can reveal itself.

It's relaxation that first allows the sensations of the body to make their presence felt and known. It's relaxation that then allows you to continue holding the gaze of your friend as, over time, ever more intensified sensations come rushing to the surface, flooding your awareness, testing your ability to continue free-falling into the contact of the gaze.

If the sensations become too intense and unusual for you to

continue to relax into them, you'll need to look away momentarily and break the contact with your friend. No worries. When you return, your friend will still be there waiting for you, smiling, patient, reeling you back in, time and time again, just as you'll still be there for your friend if he or she ever feels the need to dry off from your shared dip into the waters of union and withdraw temporarily from the intensity of the practice:

> *Thousands of times I ran away from you*
> *Like an arrow is thrown from the bow,*
> *And thousands of times I was caught again*
> *As prey by your hunting eyes.*

So relax as much as you can. Relax into the pleasurable sensations that the practice generates. Relax into the unpleasant ones as well. Make sure that the positioning of your body is as comfortable as it can possibly be and that you don't become tight or rigid as the feelings intensify. Keep monitoring the sensations of your body so that you can breathe into areas of unpleasant sensation as soon as they arise, releasing these tensions on your exhalation into all the six directions. You've finally found someone in front of whom you can relax all your defenses and just be yourself.

Acceptance

Your ability to prolong the contact of the gaze depends on your willingness to accept your experiences exactly as they appear to you, without altering or cosmeticizing them in any way. Whatever kinds of sensations you experience as you hold the gaze of your friend—whether pleasurable, unpleasant, or neutral—welcome and accept them all. If you reject your experience or attempt to manipulate or change it, the body will tighten, the mind will close down on itself, and the eyes will want to look away.

Relaxation and acceptance are like two sides of a valuable coin. You can't really separate them or have one without the other. In conjunction with each other, they create a powerful catalytic effect that supports you in going ever deeper into the practice.

As you continue with the practice, you'll want to expand your focus to include an awareness not only of the sensations inside your body, but of the sights in front of your eyes and the sounds that surround you as well. While your friend's eyes form the dual center of your roughly elliptical visual field, you can soften and broaden your gaze so that you see the whole visual field all at once. Pay as much attention to the periphery of your visual field as you ordinarily do to the primary object of interest that sits right in the center of that field. Feel how the body immediately relaxes. Then, you can bring awareness to the sounds that are present, treating each individual sound, no matter how loud or subtle, as an intrinsic component in the overall symphony of sound that the orchestra of life is playing for you in this moment.

At those moments when you're able to hold the awareness of your primary sensory fields in balance, accepting their contents exactly as they are, the internal monologue of the mind magically shuts itself off. The mind's ongoing chatter creates a powerful force field that bars your immersion in the waters of union, and so even a momentary respite is a welcome event. If your equilaterally balanced awareness of sensations, vision, and sound falters, the mind will reassert itself, and you will need, as best you can, to include the awareness of this mental activity as well.

The birthright home of union is not a castle in the clouds. It's as real as anything that exists. Because it is to be found deep at the core of your being, all you need to do is to keep on relaxing into yourself, accepting whatever occurs as a result of continuing to hold the gaze of your friend. You are not trying to change anything about yourself or to get anywhere other than where you find yourself in the present moment. The doors to the land of union don't come open through prying and forcing, but through a deep relaxation into what you can experience right now and an acceptance of the truth of that experience.

If you have pain in your body, you accept that. If waves of tingling pleasure and sensations of floating course through your body, you accept that. Accept the visual field exactly as it appears to you, letting go of any insistence that it look a certain way. Accept all the sounds just as they too appear, pushing none of them away, nor trying to hold on to any of them.

Acceptance is the key to happiness.

Accept yourself exactly as you are. Feel what's happening to you in this moment of communion with your friend, exactly as it is. Never succumb to the self-hating trap of thinking that you're inadequate, that God must have been away on holiday when you were born, that something at your core is in need of fixing, and that the repair shop is permanently closed. Rumi addressed this with compassion:

> *You suppose that you're the trouble,*
> *But you're really the cure.*
> *You suppose that you're the lock on the door,*
> *But you're really the key that opens it.*
>
> *It's too bad that you want to be someone else.*
> *You don't see your own face, your own beauty.*
> *Yet, no one's face is more beautiful than yours.*

Surrender

If you're able to relax in the presence of your great friend, accepting whatever occurs as a result of the practice, you begin to realize one of the most important truths about the world of union: everything within its domain is constantly changing in an unending parade of appearances. Nothing stands still for a single moment. Nothing lasts longer than a heartbeat. Sounds come and go. The visual field subtly shimmers. Sensations in the body are extraordinarily evanescent, like distant lights flickering on and off, altering their form from microsecond to microsecond. At the core of your being, you are a process in constant motion, shape-shifting on the fluctuating tides of change.

If you try to resist this current of change, if you attempt to freeze any momentary manifestation of experience and preserve it, the world of union will slip through your fingers and mock you for your efforts. If you learn how to swim among the surges and swells, making peace with the fluctuating appearances that are constantly coming and going, union takes you in its hand. Even though you swim and float in a sea of impermanence, you needn't fear these waters nor fight with their currents. Just enjoy them, and surrender to their ebbs and flows.

As you get more and more familiar with the fluid environment of the practice, you will soon realize that the sensations of the body are animated by a palpable, organic, and completely natural current. Just like a current in a river, it can be felt to move in its own directions and flow at its own pace. It lazes along one moment then races over waterfalls the next. Your job is simply to surrender to the current as completely as possible, to become like a leaf in a stream. You need to steer and direct the practice only so far as is necessary to contact the feeling of this current. Then you relax, let go, and go along for the ride, trusting fully in the wisdom of the current, allowing it to take you wherever it will, knowing that wherever you are taken is exactly where you need to go:

> We are like bowls floating on the surface of
>   water.
> How the bowls go is not determined by the
>   bowls but by the water.

Feeling the current of this river, you know you're alive. Surrendering to this current, you surrender to the life force itself. What a joy! If the current takes you into deeply dissolved and ecstatic eddies, you go there. If the current draws deeply embedded emotional or physical pains to the surface, you accept those too. If you can keep accepting whatever washes ashore, treasure chests and debris alike, the mind begins to melt, and the painful knots in the body begin to unravel themselves.

Painful sensations are like a logjam in a river. When painful sensations arise, feel into the very middle of them and contact the current that's being resisted there. Surrender to the current, to whatever you've been holding back from, and watch the mass of painful sensation begin to break apart. If you can kindle an awareness of a sensation and then accept it exactly as it appears, it paradoxically begins to change its shape; it transforms itself on its own. If you brace yourself against feeling a sensation or forcibly attempt to alter it, you only succeed in enshrining it, far beneath the surface of your awareness, as a permanent fixture in your being. In shielding ourselves from unpleasant sensation, we only succeed in making sure that it never leaves.

Surrender to the breath that wants to breathe you. Logjams in the body and mind can exist only when the current of the breath is being resisted.

Surrender to your partner. Don't hold anything back or keep anything hidden; on the other hand, don't try to manufacture anything either. Just surrender to the truth of who you are in this moment of communion, and surrender to all the ways that the reality of this moment changes.

◈

We are, at our core, the ocean itself, but all too often we forget this and submit to a dry and brittle life in the world of separation. If relaxation, acceptance, and surrender together comprise the money that buys us admission to the world of union, then tension, the rejection of experience, and the willful attempt to manipulate the objects of experience make up the counterfeit currency that binds us to the world of separation. Like a skilled doctor of the soul, Rumi acknowledges our condition and offers up the antidote as well:

> *Why have you turned into a dry branch?*
> *Look at the face of the Beloved.*

So much spontaneous healing can occur as you continue to gaze into each other's eyes. Pains that you've suppressed or perhaps never even knew existed suddenly rise up to the surface in a wave of energy. Then, with no effort on your part, through the magical triad of relaxation, acceptance, and surrender, the wave passes through you and the pains begin to resolve themselves. The practice of gazing at the beloved is a healing practice, healing the mind of its misconceptions, healing the body of its discomforts and pains. The medication that we most need is found in the eyes of our friend:

> *The glowing eyes of this doctor dispense remedies.*
> *Whoever is ill should come to this pharmacy.*

Don't we all suffer from the disease of the eye? Doesn't our residency in the world of separation cause our hearts to weep, often silently, sometimes openly? Rumi wrote:

> *He said to me, "Why are your eyes so fixed on*
> *my face?"*
> *I answered, "Because my eyes so wet with tears*
> *search for the heat of the sun."*

Through gazing at our beloved friend, we dry our inner tears. Through this ultimately intimate act of friendship, we enter together into a healing chamber. We enable our friend to be seen fully, and we feel that we too, finally, are being seen for who we are. When we are seen and acknowledged at this depth of being, it feels somehow safer to come out of hiding, to reveal everything that we may have been afraid to feel and show. Through giving ourselves permission to feel our body's sensations in all their many shades and textures, we give our friend permission to do the same.

> *Friend sits by Friend,*
> *And the tablets appear.*

On these tablets are written the truth of our lives. On these tablets are inscribed our joys and happiness, our greatness of spirit, as well as our sorrows and pains, our foolishness and our fears. What a thrill and relief to part the curtain that has kept all of this hidden from sight and to reveal it to another, to share ourselves as we are in truth rather than to keep fearfully believing that we need to keep our true nature concealed. The way that we heal ourselves of our shame, our insane belief that something about us is not quite right, is to share ourselves with another exactly as we are. Paradoxically, it's when we realize that we're perfectly okay as we are that we truly begin to transform.

How can we possibly look at another if our underlying motivation is to hide? By constantly averting our gaze in the world of separation, we behave like bumper cars in an amusement park. We either collide with and bounce off of each other or swerve to avoid any contact at all. And then we become lonely because we aren't able to feel the fundamental connection that we share with everyone. Between the extremes of bouncing off of other beings and swerving away altogether, there exists the real prospect of genuine contact and intimacy, of truly sharing our selves, merging as friends into the great ground of union. It's very difficult to experience that merging alone, however. For this, we need a lover's help:

Borrow the beloved's eyes!

Don't feel ashamed to make this request. Asking this of your friend is as great a gift as you could ever offer anyone. Ask him or her, "Could I borrow your eyes for a moment, please? And, besides, if you let me borrow yours, then I can let you borrow mine!"

In order for the tablets of truth to appear, the door that ordinarily keeps us isolated and separate from others needs to be opened. We achieve this through inserting our key into the lock of our friend while our friend simultaneously inserts his or her key into our lock. The key that we offer each other is the permission to accept ourselves as we truly are, to relax into our sensations in the presence of the other, to let go and yield to the current of the life force, allowing it to take us wherever it will. It can feel enormously liberating to be in the presence of someone who gives us full permission to be ourselves, to accept ourselves in all our flavors and guises, and allow the knots of shame and fear to loosen their hold, unravel, and finally come undone.

The key to opening this door is given to those who are courageous enough to become truly sensational beings. I don't refer to rock stars, movie stars, or sports heroes, but rather to ordinary men and women who can accept themselves as they truly are. These sensational beings experience the reality of their body and soul as a subtle field of shimmering tactile sensations that goes on forever, a field of dreams made real. If, with the help of the practice, you and your great friend are able to do this simultaneously, then your keys slide into each other's locks, and the door that hides the tablets springs open.

You'll know that this is happening when you begin to feel the river of sensations coursing through your body suddenly flow right into the river of sensations coursing through your beloved's body. You begin, literally and palpably, to merge with your great friend into a single, common, shared realm of experience. Where formerly you were two separate small rivers, now you meet at the point of confluence, and a single, larger river is spontaneously created. This is a true meeting of souls:

> My soul dissolves in you, and with you is
> mingled.

When you truly meet another in this way, at the depth of your souls, you both pass over the threshold of separation and find yourselves swimming together in the ocean of union. Where formerly there were two separate beings, two separate minds, two separate souls, now suddenly there is a merger into a larger being. The waters of this sea are comforting beyond any ocean you've ever bathed in.

This merging back together into a shared dimension of union is accompanied by a feeling that runs unchecked through your entire body as though the lock of a canal had been fully opened and all the water were rushing freely through. This feeling is as unmistakable and natural as was the initial sensation of contact that occurred in the middle of your heads when you and your beloved friend first sat down and laid eyes on each other. The door of union opens wide and reveals a whole new vista that neither of you may have ever seen. Thoughts dissolve, the body relaxes, and something deep inside of you opens:

> You knock at the door of reality,
> Shake your thought-wings,
> Loosen your shoulders,
> And open.

The only way to open and walk through that door is hand in hand with your beloved friend. It's not possible for one of you to enter while the other lingers on the other side of the threshold. You enter together, or not at all:

> The beauty of Love is the merger
> Of the lover with the Beloved.
> Come on now! Mix each other
> Like butter and flour,
> Just like thick soup
> Which can't be separated.

At this point in the practice, you will feel as though your soul and sensations are completely intermingled with the soul and sensations of your friend. It may even become difficult to differentiate between what must be your soul, your sensations, and what must be your friend's. You may feel as though you were pouring yourself right into, or even through, your friend's body, and then the current may organically shift, and suddenly you feel your friend's presence flooding into you, washing the protective fences of your separateness away. In this way, you and your friend function as funnels for both of you to pour yourselves into God. Like liquid that's being poured from a small container into a larger one, you pour all of yourself right through the funnel of your friend into the larger bottle of God, and not a single drop is spilled on the counter.

Just as you initially worked to familiarize yourself with the tidal flows of your own body's sensations, now you need to learn to surrender to the current of these new waters, composed of the blending of your sensations and your soul with those of your friend's. Where formerly there were two separate rivers, now there's only one. When you and your beloved friend become as one, then a whole other dimension of being comes, as Rumi says, from the formerly invisible and unseen world:

Whenever two are linked this way,
There comes Another from the unseen world.

Rumi often refers to the appearance of this new shared being with a capital letter: the friends meet, and the Friend appears. Sometimes, this appearance can occur immediately, as soon as you sit down to practice with your beloved friend. Other times, it may take many hours, or even days or weeks. If the tablets don't appear immediately, do not fret. Just continue doing the practice, and they eventually will:

If He is not in your eye,
If His image does not immediately appear
*   before your eyes,*
Still, look for Him with patience.
Stay in the eye.

The capital-H person that Rumi is referring to is the shared consciousness that emerges through the merging of you and your friend. Have patience. Gazing at the beloved is not like eating fast food. While a few moments of practice or even a simple glance between you and your beloved friend can release a hint of the aroma of the food of union, you can truly appreciate its taste only through sitting down for a long and unhurried meal.

When you first begin the practice, you and your friend will very likely go through an initial period of awkwardness in which the mind of separation resists its inevitable destruction, pulling back from its destiny as it has always done. Wait patiently. Stay in the eye, and the tablets your soul searches for will eventually appear. As soon as true contact begins to occur between the two of you, as soon as your souls and sensations begin to merge, the awkwardness vanishes, and suddenly it feels as though you could sit at this table and enjoy this meal for days on end.

Friend sits by Friend,
And the tablets appear.
They read the mysteries off each other's forehead.

The mysteries that appear are not carved in stone, like the laws on the tablets that Moses brought down from the mountain. They appear, rather, more like the burning bush, as a dazzling light show in which the familiar visible world loses its hard edges and begins to shimmer and melt. In the practice of gazing at the beloved, both the way that you see and what you see undergo dramatic alterations. At first, it may feel as though you were seeing not out of the physical eyes in your head but from a place both behind and beneath your physical eyes. At other times, it may feel as though you were looking not just with your eyes, but with the whole of the body, as though the body itself had become the organ of vision:

I became totally eyes from head to feet.

In addition to this shifting of the locus of vision, you may experience a condition that the prophet Muhammad called *ma zagha*, a way of looking in which "the eyes do not roam." Rumi, too, speaks of the eyes keeping still:

The mystery does not get clearer by repeating
  the question,
Nor is it bought with going to amazing places.

Until you've kept your eyes
And your wanting still for fifty years,
You don't begin to cross over from confusion.

In gazing at the beloved, the eyes become quite still. They don't dart around as they do when you dream and, through the practice, you come out of the frightening dream of separation to be soothed in the maternal arms of union. When the eyes are still and don't roam, the mind too becomes still and doesn't roam. A doorway then appears (it was there all the time, that clear bead at the center, but it was concealed behind the cloudier activity of the mind's chatter), and you can walk right through it out into the landscape of union.

Even more dramatic, the visual field that you look out onto may begin to change its appearance in the most unusual and startling ways. If you're able to experience the whole of your body as an effulgent field of shimmering sensations, then the visual field begins to shimmer and glow as well. The hard edges of your friend's face and form may begin to soften and become less delineated. You may experience reversals in light as though his or her face were becoming a photographic negative of itself rather than the printed picture. You may see colors or a glowing light surrounding your friend.

And, then, the features of his or her face may metamorphose and change right before your eyes, like a plastic figurine melting in a fire, until a whole different being is sitting in front of you. Your friend may suddenly look like an angelic being, a young child, a creature from another planet, a recognizable figure from history or popular culture, your aunt Rose. Different feeling states and personae may also express themselves through your friend's shifting face. An innocent boy, a shy girl, a disturbed youth, an unconditionally loving elder, a terrified adult: the permutations and possibilities are endless.

At times, it's clear that the person you see sitting in front of you is a hidden aspect of your friend that he or she rarely shows to anyone. At other times, it may almost seem as though you were with a completely different being from the one you think you know your friend to be, perhaps a person from a different place and a different time. And at other times still, you're not seeing your friend at all but meeting instead some aspect of yourself, perhaps unknown, as though your friend's face had become a Rorschach blot onto which you project your own deepest mysteries. Face after face appears before you. Don't try to hold your friend to any one appearance. You couldn't do so even if you wanted to. Just relax into the passing show in front of you:

> *What disguises he wears, what tricks he invents!*
> *If he appears in one shape, as spirit he slips the snare.*
> *When you seek him above, he shines like the*
>   *moon in water;*
> *When you enter the water, he flees skyward.*

In the beginning, it may seem as though you'd both entered into an altered state of consciousness, a hallucinatory world with visions not unlike those associated with the ingestion of psychotropic drugs. However, if you can surrender into the visual shifts and distortions that are a natural by-product of the practice without feeling that you need to resurrect the form of the visible world with which you're more familiar, then the current of the ocean of union will continue to sweep you along, revealing ever deeper mysteries as you go.

From this perspective, the world that passes as normal is suddenly seen as the altered state, and indeed it truly is altered. Instead of relaxing completely into the felt presence of our bodies and minds, we normally alter and manipulate our experience. We withhold sensations. We hide our thoughts and impulses out of shame. We squeeze and tense the energies and muscles in our bodies to create a desired identity: a confident raconteur with an unlimited repertoire of stories, a successful wheeler-dealer intent on establishing his status, a seductive enchantress, a tough cookie with street smarts and attitude to match. The practice of gazing at the beloved takes us from the limited altered state of our multiple created identities back into our birthright, our natural condition as God.

Sometimes, in a condition of the deepest union and merging, the whole of your friend's face may dissolve, all of his or her features melting, and all that you see in front of you is a single eye:

When his bright face becomes an eye
To humans' eyes,
Humans are able to see God.

And then, even the eyes may dissolve into a kind of blank, but blinding light. The visible world of form and appearance with which we're so familiar, the cornerstone of what we believe reality to be and look like, may suddenly disappear, and another world beyond the world of form reveals its face:

You turned into eyes.
Then we both became invisible.

As you continue to surrender ever more deeply into the practice, your friend's forehead becomes a makeshift cinema screen on which a movie of the most spectacular mysteries (sometimes an action adventure, sometimes an emotional drama, sometimes a sci-fi spectacle, and sometimes a hilarious comedy) is being projected. Rumi tells us, however, not to expect that we can view such a movie by lining up politely at a Saturday matinee. The visions and feeling states of the world of union are available only to friends and lovers who become completely intoxicated on the wine that they pour into each other through their gazing, friends and lovers who can't stand up anymore, but reach for another bottle anyway. The price of admission to this movie is one's sobriety:

For God's sake, don't ask for the taste
Of this wine from the sober ones.

The favors that this wine bestows are to be
found in the eyes of drunkards.

The practice of gazing at the beloved is for people who are completely drunk on each other, whose love of the practice is so acute that others, who don't understand this thirst for God would label the two friends' need to keep their gaze fixed on each other as obsessional. To these people, Rumi simply says:

Nobody but the blind asks me
To turn my face from the Beloved.

In a more conciliatory passage, Rumi explains this behavior more clearly to those who remain perplexed by the change in character that the practice sometimes effects:

The one you call crazy
Is not really crazy.
He's giving birth to his soul.
That's why he keeps his eyes so fixed on his
* Beloved.*

Gazing at the beloved is a practice of surrender in tandem, a bicycle to God built for two. Both riders must stay equally focused on riding the bike, or it will topple over and fall to the ground. Learning how to ride such a bicycle gives back lost respectability to obsession. Understand, however, that this is no ordinary obsession, like a newfound passion for figs and filberts. Gazing at the beloved provides an opening to the fullest and deepest energies that are available to a human body. It reveals the mysteries that you most long to discover, in endless succession, literally before your eyes. Isn't it only sane to become obsessed with such a practice?

The beauty of that Arab caught my mind and
   my heart.
There were thousands of amazing things
In his drunken eyes.

In several poems, Rumi refers to Shams's eyes as "magic eyes," and, indeed, there does appear to be much magic in the practice as the world of separation is transformed into the world of union, again, right before your eyes. This is true alchemical magic, the transformation of two pieces of common lead into a single shared nugget of gold. And yet there are no tricks here, no sleight of hand, no palming of cards, no pigeons concealed underneath a magician's robes, no bunnies pulled from a hat. This is the real thing. The greatest act of magic is the reclamation of your birthright. It's also the most natural thing that could ever happen to you if, as Rumi insists, you're truly a drunkard for union:

Both our eyes became drunk with the glass
Of the greatest of the great vintages,
   Shamseddin.
What wines there are at the eyes, what wines!

Who or what is this indwelling presence that lives inside your looking and shows its face when you and your beloved friend gaze at each other for unbroken hours at a time? Rumi knows the answer to this question, and he tells us:

The patron of your eyes is God,
Who is always alive and creating constantly.

Through this act of mutual creation, God comes alive in you and your partner. The practice of gazing at the beloved can be looked upon as a ritual ceremony in which the participants enter together into a sacred dyad and offer themselves up to God as a human sacrifice. Through surrendering their personal will to the will of God, friends in the practice allow this great energy to move through them however it wants to. This is true worship:

> The importance of eye and sight
> Is to give praise and thanks to God.

Could it possibly be that our constant turning away from one another, the miserly and fearful withholding of our gaze, is the one simple act that causes us not to see everything as God? For when we truly look, many of the familiar concepts about reality that the mind of separation clings to for support suddenly appear quite shaky and may even come tumbling down. Once the dust settles, we look out onto a different world, one in which everything shimmers and glows and appears inextricably related to everything else.

When asked how best to decipher the puzzle of reality, the philosopher Ludwig Wittgenstein is reported to have replied: "Don't think. Look!" Only those who give themselves permission to look and see become seers and visionaries. They see what's truly here to be seen and realize that there's more to meet the eye than we conventionally suppose.

The practice is really so simple. Sit down with your great friend. Gaze at each other. Open to the feelings that the gaze brings to life. Then, relax and surrender into the play of light and sensations as you and your friend are swept away together into the commingled waters of union. Those are really all the instructions you need. The practice itself then becomes your further guide:

> Look at the drunken eyes of the person
> Who drank early morning wine from that cupbearer.
> You'll understand the rest of it.

The longer you and your friend sit together, holding each other's gaze and letting the current of the life force move through you, the deeper will you both descend into the cavern of union. Rumi and Shams spent months together. Maybe you and your friend won't be able to spend that much time. But hopefully you can spend hours together or, perhaps on special occasions, even days and weeks. The energies of God are not sprinters at the Olympics but prefer to reveal their secrets at a slower and more leisurely pace. Nor do they respond to an imposed timetable, showing up promptly at eight in the morning and leaving at five that afternoon. They are always here and available, but if they're rushed in any way, they simply won't show up.

Because the practice takes you so deeply into an awareness of the present moment, time may feel distorted. You may feel as though you and your friend had been sitting together for fifty minutes only to look at a watch and realize that two hours have passed. More can happen in those two hours than sometimes happens in two weeks of a life. As with any practice, if you want to get good at it, you need to devote time to it. Do you want what the practice offers?

> *His soul is a mirror that reflects the beauty of God.*
> *His eye is a glass that reveals the mysteries*
> *At the meeting of lovers.*
>
> *Whoever drinks the wine of secrets from this*
>   *glass*
> *Will be annihilated at the union with the Beloved.*
> *He will go beyond himself with ecstasy.*

If this is what you want for yourself, then stay looking at your friend for as long as you can. Minutes flow into hours. Hours may flow into days and weeks.

But, be forewarned. The practice is highly addictive. Once you taste its pleasures, you may want to do little else. Just as it was initially awkward to enter into the practice, it may now feel awkward to leave it, to sever the contact, to move away from your friend, and to enter back into your distantly remembered life:

> *We are looking at your face.*
> *Meadows and rose gardens don't interest us anymore.*
> *We are lost in the view of your eyes.*
> *Wine and the wine maker no longer have appeal.*

Union is like that. Until you take it fully in your mouth, you may shy away from it, like an exotic food from another part of the world, marinated in spices foreign to your tongue. The familiar fare and daily bread of separation may appear much more attractive and palatable than this strange-looking dish sitting before you. But once you truly taste it, you instantly understand what you've been missing. Then, the familiar meadows and rose gardens of your life, the local wines that you've grown up with, seem suddenly less appealing. Your enjoyment of them begins to dissolve and disappear, like snow melting in the sun.

Rumi speaks of the dissolving into union, the ultimate mystery, as an annihilation. If you're attached to the mind that views itself as an "I," separate and distinct from everything that exists outside of the body in which it resides, such a prospect sounds terrifying, the very death of what you believe yourself to be. But if you've tasted the sweetmeat of union, relishing how it dissolves in your mouth and how you dissolve into it, then talk of this annihilation is music to your ears. By giving up your separate sense of self, even if only momentarily, you gain your participation in the whole world.

Such a trade is not for the weak of heart or the prudish of spirit. It's for lovers of God who want their love to be orgasmic, lovers of God who exult in the feeling of dissolving beyond themselves, lovers of God who are spiritual gluttons, lovers of God who fall asleep in love, completely spent and sated, and who wake in the early morning hours hungry for more:

> *My eyes have wet dreams*
> *In the early dawn*
> *When they meet yours.*

5

Language of the Heart

*T*he Sufis have a beautiful word for the mystical communion that two openhearted practitioners can enter into when they come into each other's presence. They call this communion and sharing *sohbet*. Essentially untranslatable, the word has most often been thought of as an extended mystical conversation in which two seekers after God come together and speak openly to each other about mystical matters. However, in the purest sohbet, words are not used as the medium of communication. While words remain the perfect currency for transacting the business of this world, the primary language of the heart is silence.

The practice of gazing at the beloved is the ultimate expression of sohbet. You and your friend may find yourselves sitting silently together for long hours without ever uttering a single word, and yet volumes of unspoken communications may pass back and forth between you. And so, Rumi tells us:

Be silent.
If someone tells you there is no speech possible
Without words or sounds,
Don't listen to him. It's not true.

Be silent.
Without the bread of God
And the wine of annihilation, that word and that
Alphabet are like two or three empty cups at best.

Be silent.
Speak the meaning without the alphabet
If you can.
Say it without words, so the heart
Can take over the conversation.

If you can learn the alphabet of the heart's language, then you can decipher the messages and communications that are written on the unprinted pages of your friend's face. If you can learn how to speak in the language of the heart, then you can communicate to your friend everything that your heart needs to share and express.

When *Friend sits by Friend, / And the tablets appear,* the mysteries reveal themselves in endless succession. This is best accomplished wordlessly through the silent language of feelings. For example, an unexpected energy, like a sudden gust of wind, may move through your friend and transform him or her before your eyes into a beautiful angel or, perhaps, a frightened little child. Your friend relaxes and allows the energies to move through; you relax and receive the beloved as he or she is. No words are necessary. Both of you know exactly what's going on.

Rumi and Shams must have spent long unbroken periods gazing at each other without a single word ever being spoken, and yet they came to know each other in a way and at a depth that few of us ever touch. Only they could know the true nature of what was transpiring between them. To an outsider looking in, it must have all appeared very secretive and mysterious indeed:

> *All our lives we've looked*
> *Into each other's faces.*
> *That was the case today too.*
> *How do we keep our love a secret?*
> *We speak from brow to brow*
> *And hear with our eyes.*

While the mastery of language lends an undeniable power to the actions of our lives, words alone can't come anywhere close to expressing the richness of union. Try as we might, we succeed only in confusing things if, at the moment of union, we attempt to communicate its extraordinary nature through words, for the experience of union takes us to a silent place where words don't reside:

> *Even "friend" and "beloved"*
> *Are wrong words for this.*
> *Even "ahhhhh" retreats back into my mouth*
> *Like the moon going behind a cloud.*
> *A pure silent look is better.*

When we start to talk to our friend in the midst of deep merging, even if it's about important matters relating to the heart and soul, we tend to draw back from the domain of union and become separate once again.

The technology of words, like a rusty abacus, just isn't capable of calculating the higher mathematics of the heart. A more powerful instrument is required for those computations, and it appears in the form of silence. Silence both sustains the conversation and keeps it on track. Silence clears the debris and fallen branches of the mind, forging the least-obstructed pathway that can safely guide us into and through the forest of union:

> *In the silence of our longing*
> *We are together as one.*
> *But as soon as we start talking,*
> *We separate back into two.*
> *So be silent.*
> *There is honor in silence*
> *For you and me.*

Over and over again, Rumi extols the virtues of silence as the medium through which ultimate truth can best be expressed. He chides the orators for their verbosity and views their barrage of spoken language as a curtain that serves to hide the truly important communications that need to be shared:

> *You have spent your whole life*
> *With elegant speeches.*
> *For some time you should*
> *Walk alone in the gardens of silence.*

When you and your friend sit down together for an extended period of practice, you stimulate the clear bead in the center of your heads through the power of your shared gaze. Ordinarily, we cannot see or feel this bead. Its calm presence is hidden behind the involuntary thoughts that, like untamed horses, race through our minds. But, through the practice, these involuntary thoughts of the mind are gradually released and reveal, in their place, the felt presence of the current of the life force, passing through this center of the body. Now liberated, the current washes away the obstructions and debris of the mind (which is generally so preoccupied with story lines of thought) as if clearing up a logjam from a bend in the river, leaving a freely flowing channel through which the waters of union can pass.

It's not just spoken words that Rumi is encouraging you to renounce. To enter fully into the world of union, let go of the unspoken words of the mind as well:

> *What would happen if you*
> *Gave up thought for one moment,*
> *Plunged into our sea like a fish,*
> *And swallowed the waves there?*
>
> *Give them up.*
> *You will be one of the Ashab-i Kehf*
> *And turn into a holy light,*
> *Silent, exempt from thought.*
> *Why don't you become like this?*

Ordinarily, we think that we couldn't live without the constant commentary of the internal monologue of our minds. Its words and thoughts are the lifeblood that fuels our belief in our existence as individual beings, separate from the rest of reality in which we live. Lost in thought, we are each like the lord living in a manor on a high hill, removed from the tumult of the town in the valley below. But the lord's life may become a lonely one, and his heart may begin to close. His thoughts insulate him, just like the walls surrounding his estate, from the larger and richer life of his heart. If, one day, he can rise above his thoughts, a great opening can occur in his heart, and then he may lower the bridges on the moat around his manor, invite the whole of the town to an open house, and begin the party of his life.

As most spiritual practitioners so well understand, calming the thoughts of the mind can be a dauntingly challenging assignment.

But the practice of gazing at the beloved powerfully supports your efforts in this important task. When you hold the gaze of your great friend, you naturally become more aware of the sensations in your body. Thoughts and sensations are like two children in a school-yard playground sitting on opposite ends of a teeter-totter. When one of them is elevated, the other is in decline. They can't both be suspended in the air or resting on the ground at the same time. By heightening your awareness of the sensations in your body, the practice of gazing at the beloved automatically calms your mind. As the sensations increasingly fill your body, your mind gradually empties itself out.

When, through the practice, you arrive at a place that is free of superficial thoughts and words, the heart spontaneously opens, and the sohbet truly begins. At that point, the messages that most need to be communicated between you and your great friend, messages that spring from the depths of your souls, are wordlessly transmitted back and forth between you. Once the involuntary monologue of the mind becomes quiet, thoughts and awarenesses that are truly important arise naturally:

> Thought doesn't come to your mind
> Until you become quiet.
> Heart doesn't open its mouth
> Until you close yours.

In the midst of a deep gazing embrace, your bodies and minds begin to function in a very different way from how they ordinarily operate. A body that is unaware of its sensational presence and a mind that is lost in superficial thought are tuned to a lower frequency than are a body that has kindled an awareness of itself as a unified field of sensations from head to foot and a mind that has become accordingly quiet and receptive. In the practice of gazing at the beloved, you become like the quartz crystals that were used in the earliest radios, attuned to the frequencies of union and the programming of the heart. You receive the messages that the world of union transmits and broadcast them directly to your friend who sits across from you:

> The Prince rides forth to hunt in the morning:
> May our hearts be wounded by the arrow of
>   his eye!
> What messages pass between his eye and mine!
> May my eye be heartened by his embrace!

"What is that you express in your eyes?" asks the American poet Walt Whitman. "It seems to me more than all the words I have read in my life." Just stay wordlessly in the eye with your beloved friend. Stay silent, and continue to hold each other's gaze, and the energies of the heart will become liberated and communicate their secrets back and forth between you.

Words are capable of spinning tales equally of fiction and fact, but the heart never lies. It can tell only the truth, and the truth is always expressed in a person's eyes:

> Tell my secret with your eyes,
> Without lips or tongues.

Just as the mind uses words to express its thoughts, the heart expresses its truths through the waves of feeling-presence that erupt, one after the other, through the body. You can know the feeling tone of these waves—gracious, angry, gentle, sad—through the look in your friend's eyes as you hold his or her gaze, and you can decipher the hidden messages of their contents through the energies that emerge out of your friend's body and enter directly into yours. The energies of the heart are multiple and varied and present themselves in an endless series of waves.

As you sit with your friend, a feeling begins to build in your body just like an ocean wave that builds on its journey to the shore. You simply surrender to that feeling, allowing it to build and crest at its own pace, and when its energies reach a breaking point, they naturally spill over and communicate their physical presence, as well as their meaning, right into and through your friend's body and mind. Wave after wave builds, crests, crashes on the beach, and then flows back again into the ocean. Each wave is unique. Each one may bear a different message and communication. Stay in the eye, and *read the mysteries off each other's forehead,* one after the next.

One of the most common mistakes that practitioners on the path of the heart routinely make is that they may successfully open to an expression of the heart's energy, but they then try to freeze or hold that energy to that one particular manifestation. It's misleading to speak of the energy of the heart in the singular. The heart has many energies, each one a unique event. Today's manifestation of the heart, today's communications that pass from your eyes to your beloved's eyes, may be totally different from the messages of yesterday. Always stay open to whatever wants to occur and whatever needs to be expressed right now.

The energies of the heart are constantly flashing forward in an unbroken series of rushes, waves, and pulsings that you will feel in your body. By experiencing these waves moving through you, one after the other, you get back in touch with your natural state:

> *Every moment a new fountain springs from the*
> *heart,*
> *Rivers flow from your sea.*
> *Heart is blinking its eyes to your glory,*
> *To your glory.*

Once you and your friend truly taste the give-and-take of the energetic flow and movement back and forth between you during a significant sohbet, once you learn how to liberate the current of the life force and allow it to communicate its messages, you may want this unspoken conversation to continue and never end. The practice of gazing at the beloved may forever alter your understanding of the meaning of friendship. Conventional discourse may no longer hold as much appeal for you as it once did:

> *Either give me wine or leave me alone,*
> *Now that I know how it is*
> *To be with you in a constant conversation.*

Remember, above all, that there are no fixed rules to this practice. There may be times when words effortlessly flow between you and your friend, and there's nothing wrong with that. And, at times, you may become so excited that you can't help but declare your happiness in words:

> *I know I ought to be silent,*
> *But the excitement of this keeps opening*
> *My mouth just like a sneeze or a yawn!*

However, you will undoubtedly discover that your familiar reliance on words as the sole medium to communicate your thoughts and feelings actually interferes with your continued surrender into the realm of union. If you speak too much, you will keep yourself from dissolving more deeply into the warming waters of union. It's like drawing a lovely hot bath but not getting into it. In an extended sohbet, too many words and thoughts simply communicate your unwillingness to enter into communion. The veil of mind reasserts itself and keeps you from your heart's desire.

How ironic, and how lucky for us, that Rumi, who so clearly understood the futility of language to express the highest truths, nonetheless kept opening his mouth, over and over again, day after day, ranting and raving, spontaneously composing beautifully crafted songs and poems that spelled out, in great detail and vivid imagery, the glories and challenges of the spiritual life. He never wrote down any of these poems himself. He never labored over their composition, endlessly drafting and redrafting them until, as an artist, he was finally satisfied with their expression. He simply opened his mouth, and the poems recited themselves. Fortunately for us, his utterances were then recorded by a selected group of scribes known as the Secretaries of the Secret. It was they who compiled all of his writings after his death, and it is through their efforts that you and I can be moved and instructed by Jalaluddin's words today.

The poems are Rumi's gifts to us. He could not stop them from coming. Still, he must have enormously enjoyed the periods of silence that characterized his excursions into union through the long, unbroken periods of gazing at Shams and, later on in his life, at his other two great companions in the practice. It was out of the silence that the words eventually emerged, as plants emerge from the soil. In the *Mathnavi,* the great spiritual discourse that he composed late in his life, Rumi jokingly refers to the paradox of having been both a silent gazer and lover of God as well as a chatty wordsmith.

At this later stage of his life, he enjoyed entering into the sohbet with Hosamoddin Chelabi, an ascetic practitioner who had, so many years before, been one of the rare supporters of his great friendship with Shams. Hosamoddin's priorities must have been mixed, indeed. On the one hand, it was he who encouraged Rumi to compose the *Mathnavi* and preserve his thoughts on the spiritual life for the benefit of posterity. On the other hand, he was Rumi's chosen companion in the practice and must have enjoyed, more than anything, to spend silent hours gazing at his beloved friend.

Referring to Hosamoddin, Rumi jokingly alludes to this paradox:

> *I think of rhymes, but my beloved says:*
> *"Don't think of anything but my face!"*

As you continue to hold the gaze of your friend, you may not be able to say a thing. At times, the energies that the practice releases may be so powerful that all you can do is to sit dumbfounded, physically unable to open your jaw even if you had to. What, really, could you say at a moment like this anyway? What could be more important than the great news that your eyes and heart were communicating to your friend?

And what could you tell your fellow citizens when they asked you to explain what you were doing and what was transpiring between you and your friend? Perhaps, the most important communication that you could bring back to the world from your travels with your beloved to the land of union would be the simple sharing of the great nature of the practice. Through that sharing, hopefully others would be inspired to make the journey for themselves, to bask in the glories of the new sounds, sights, and feelings that silently await them there. Maybe the only appropriate thing that you could say would be something like this:

> *I have seen your unseeable beauty,*
> *And the wordless report of this vision has*
> *   reached my heart*
> *Which became all eye with the news.*
> *"Long life to eyes! Long life to eyes!"*
> *Says my heart now over and over.*

Or, if someone kept pressing you, complaining that that wasn't enough, and that they needed more specific information, more precise details to help them understand the nature of the silent communications that pass between two beloved friends when they sit gazing at each other, perhaps, like Rumi, you might explain it to them this way:

> *My drunken eyes*
> *Are talking to your eyes.*
> *What are they saying?*
> *"Take us both to Union."*

6

The Birthing River of Darkness and Light

*T*he practice of gazing at the beloved is like a float trip that takes you down the river of your soul and ends at the ocean of union. Starting off from the familiarity of dry land, you and your friend place your raft in the river, climb aboard together, and then simply surrender to the current, passing through untold adventures along the way until you arrive at your destination where the river empties itself into the ocean. And then you take the trip over and over and over again.

While it's impossible to predict the specific events and occurrences that await you, there are four main stages that you are likely to encounter on your journey. Some of these stages are filled with light, like the noonday sun on a cloudless day. Others may take you into dark moonless nights where hidden creatures crouch, waiting to jump out and scare you. Each stage is marked by a different condition of the body and the mind. Understanding these stages before you launch your raft can help prepare you for the unusual adventures and transformations that lie ahead.

The first stage is the conventional condition of the body and mind that creates the consciousness that passes as normal in the world at large. This is where we all begin the journey. Even though many good and decent people will spend their entire lives here and never proceed any further, Rumi refers to this stage as the dry and brittle land, the hardened and parched earth that removes us from the life-giving waters for which our hearts so thirst.

The civilized world in which we live, with all its very real joys and fears, is primarily a first-stage world. Whether we are victims or victors, we tend so to identify with the material forms and roles that we have been cast into that we lose touch with the animating spirit, the life force that inhabits these forms. In this first stage, we suppress the naturally expansive energies of the body and mind, as though we were turning down the dimmer switch on a lightbulb, and settle for an existence that is less luminous than it might otherwise be. Like a black hole in space that collapses down on itself and doesn't let light escape or radiate out from it, we withdraw into ourselves and effectively become separate from everything we perceive to exist outside of our bodies. The first stage enshrines the perspective of separation as the reigning consciousness of choice.

As inhabitants of the first stage, we protect ourselves from feeling the full vibrancy of our bodily life through the creation of a subtle, but pervasive pattern of numbing tension that blankets our body from head to foot. But like deer that somehow manage to get into a fenced garden and nibble away at the vegetables, pockets of pain still manage to poke through this protective barrier and eat away at our peace of mind.

When the vibrant life of the body is compromised in this way, the mind, too, forfeits its natural openness and radiance and collapses in on itself. The internal monologue of the mind, the voice that speaks to us inside our head, begins to spew forth its silent running commentary on every aspect of our life, telling and retelling its stories of fear and hope for the future, of failures and conquests of the past, until even we become bored with its pronouncements. The speaker of this monologue is this mysterious character named "I," and the egoistic orientation of this most conventional aspect of the mind powerfully reinforces our belief in separation. The "I" is always known only in contrast to everything that it perceives itself not to be, and that means the whole of the perceptible world that exists outside of the body.

In this first stage, you are an island, separate and distinct from the ocean that surrounds you on all sides. Of all the many behavioral ploys that help secure your residency in the first stage, one above all warrants mention: here, people will rarely ever look directly at one another and will avert their gaze quickly if their eyes inadvertently chance to meet.

While many people manage to turn a deaf ear to the call of the waters that beckon them to move beyond the insular life of the first stage, the Sufi hears that call as a loud stirring within his or her soul and feels it as a pressure deep within the heart. Know that the tugging pain that you may feel in the pit of your heart is not a sign that something is amiss with you. That pain is your thirsty heart calling out for water and, even better yet, for the sacred wine that Rumi encourages you to drink to excess. It's a sign that the protective strategies designed to keep you relatively happy behind the dikes that surround the land of separation are beginning to corrode and break down. Just as the waters in a river feel the tug of gravity pulling them downward toward their ultimate merging with the ocean, the tug that you feel in your heart is the longing to reconnect with the beloved from whom you feel separated. The dark pains that inevitably appear when you're ready to move beyond the first stage are what push you to leave the dry land of separation behind, launch your raft, and move on in your journey. These dark pains are like contractions of labor that give birth to the Sufi in you.

Now, to complicate matters, the entrance to the river on which you hope to launch your raft is not visible to the eye from your ordinary perspective! Because of the deeply ingrained cultural taboo against the experience of union, we've learned not to look to the one place that unfailingly leads to that river. Certainly, we've looked everywhere else, and the scientists among us continue to create ever more sophisticated instruments of vision that let them artificially peer into the farthest reaches of space as well as into the core of the smallest particles. But we still shy away from looking with our naked eyes at what is directly in front of us, as though our human vision were not to be trusted. Like the characters searching for the invisible portal leading to the sacred mountain in René Daumal's *Mount Analogue,* seekers on the path of the heart must somehow figure out how to find the invisible way back to this river.

And here is where an understanding of the practice of gazing at the beloved is so helpful, for it leads us to the invisible opening through which we can fall into the river, launch our raft, and begin our journey. That opening, that portal that allows us to leave the world of separation behind and enter into the waters that will take us all the way to the ocean of union, appears in the eyes of our beloved friend. As we gaze at our friend, the hard edges of the world of separation begin to soften, a crack between the two worlds opens up, and we can fall right through, just like Alice falling through the looking glass into Wonderland. As Rumi put it:

> *An unseen well can be found*
> *In the valley of your friend's face.*
> *Go to that valley,*
> *And try to fall into that well.*

The transition between the first and second stages is often marked by the initial awkwardness that you and your friend may feel when you first sit down and begin to look at each other. The consciousness of the first stage lingers, the consciousness of the second stage beckons, and you feel momentarily caught between the pull of these two opposing forces. Some people abandon the journey at this point and retreat to the safe and familiar haven of dry land.

But, if you can keep on relaxing the body and the mind while you continue to fall into the eyes of your friend, the awkwardness lifts like a fog that's burned off by the heat of the sun. You may begin to feel a comfort unlike anything you've ever felt before as it grows and spreads throughout your entire body and mind, until you become completely engulfed in its warm caress. It's like warily setting sail on rough waters and then suddenly finding your sea legs. The small raft in which you and your friend ride begins to move gracefully and easily through the flowing waters, floating freely, fully buoyant, and you're transported into the second stage.

The second stage is like the first *satori* in Zen, the first glimpse or foretaste of the salty waters of union that await you farther along in your journey. It can be sublimely pleasurable and very bright. The numbness and pain of the body are transformed into gentle sensations of tingling and streaming. It's like something waking up in your body, a cat stretching after a long nap. You begin to feel the fluid currents of change moving right through you and your beloved friend in an organic series of sensual waves. The internal monologue of the mind, on the other hand, may go into a sleepy hibernation and shut itself down. In its place, feelings of great love, joy, and happiness may flood your body and mind, radiating their warmth to and through your friend. The second stage of the journey is always exciting, as welcome as the sun that appears after forty days and nights of a cold rain. It's also very seductive.

Leaving the flat and dry land of the first stage behind and

entering joyously into the second stage of your journey is cause for real celebration. Your body and mind become much lighter. The barriers of separation that have kept you isolated, an island unto yourself, begin to break down, and you have your first taste of merging with your friend into a shared realm of love. Most people, upon tasting the happiness of the second stage, would like to live here forever. A profound feeling of gratitude for having encountered the practice and a genuine understanding of the principles and power of relaxation, acceptance, and surrender may wash over you and carry both you and your friend effortlessly along.

It's easy to settle into the joy of floating down a river in paradise, meandering along peacefully, the sun shining pleasurably on your body, the water refreshing you, spectacular foliage and brightly colored birds on both banks of the river, the mind empty, the body glowing. But what happens when suddenly you round a bend in the river, and there, right in front of you, completely blocking your way, covering the whole width and expanse of the river, is a wall of fire with only the tiniest opening in the middle? What will you do now? Will you recoil in horror, turn the raft around, and start paddling furiously back upstream, against the current, back to where everything had been so beautiful? Will you steer the raft to shore and bring the journey to a halt while you wait for help or try to devise a clever strategy to bypass the ring of fire? Will you dissolve your friendship, convincing yourself that your friend wasn't the right person with whom to embark on this journey in the first place? Or, recognizing that a float trip that doesn't take you through a series of chutes and rapids that scare you silly probably isn't a trip worth taking, will you continue to surrender to the current, allowing it to sweep you right into the mouth of the blaze? Whatever your response, you've just reached the third stage of your journey.

The third stage may come on very quickly and unexpectedly. You may be sitting with your friend, feeling the energies of your bodies merging and intermingling, awash in a sense of intimate wonder and love. Then everything changes in the blink of an eye, and for no apparent reason you begin to feel extremely insecure and unlovable, desperate for attention and affection, free-falling into despair, terrified of the austere figure sitting across from you. Or perhaps your body is shimmering with a glow and comfort that you've never before experienced, when suddenly the feeling starts growing larger, and then larger still, too large for its container, and you feel as though a volcano were about to erupt through the wall of your chest and you can hardly breathe through the pressure. What will you do? Can you surrender to these new sensations and feelings with the same acceptance and equanimity with which you greeted the beauties and glories of the more gentle and comforting portion of the river through which you've just passed?

Rumi's words clearly illustrate that the journey back to the ocean of union is fraught with challenge and peril; it is not just a pleasant dip in a cooling stream. Darkness and fear are as likely to be your companions on this journey as are shining light and ease. Such is the nature of the third stage. You may encounter dense and viscous layers of tension deep at the core of your body that you never even knew existed. The aches and pains that you now feel can make the aches and pains of the first stage appear almost trivial in comparison.

Indeed, the third stage of the journey possesses an octave relationship to the first stage, at the levels of both body and mind. The mind, so clear and carefree a moment earlier, can become once again filled with thought forms and flooded with images of negativity. You may feel hopeless, depressed, terrified, raging, or filled with a sadness whose tears have no end. The bright daylight of the second stage, now just a cruel and distant memory, feels as though it had retreated forever behind an eternal cloud, and you find yourself plunked down right in the middle of what has traditionally been called the dark night of the soul. Nobody wants this stage of the journey. Everybody, to a greater or lesser degree, experiences it.

It's extremely important to understand that the appearances of the third stage are an essential and completely natural part of the journey and that it is necessary to pass through their challenges. There are no ways around this ring of fire, this monolith of pain and confusion, this beast with its mouth wide open, its teeth bared, waiting expectantly to receive you just like the whale into which Jonah was swallowed. As in the lyrics to the gospel hymn "Rock My Soul," this monolithic obstruction is so high you can't climb over it, it descends so deep beneath the surface of the river that you can't possibly dive under it, it's so wide that there's no way that you can portage around it. There is only one way to get through and past it. You need to enter right into its fiery mouth. The nurturing mother of the second stage becomes the mother that tosses her children into the fires of purification. The Virgin Mary turns into the goddess Kali.

Many religious paths and traditions, like business ventures that would prefer that you not read the fine print, are shamefully irresponsible in not preparing their practitioners beforehand for the inevitable passage through the third stage of the journey. They would like you to believe that, if you just keep following the precepts of the teachings, everything will just keep getting happier and lighter. Certainly, this is what we all want to hear. The ego-based mind wants to get itself out of the boredom and discomfort of the first stage and take up residence in the pleasures of the second, but it doesn't want the journey to continue, as it inevitably must, into the third stage.

However, trying to make your residency in the second stage a permanent one can't possibly work and, even if it could, it couldn't ultimately satisfy you. The current is eventually going to evict you and propel you onward in your journey whether you want it to or not. Only by passing through the third stage can the dark night and egoistic orientation of the mind be sufficiently dismantled so that the sun of union might dawn upon you in the ensuing morning; not until this occurs will your heart arrive at the object of its true desire.

Rumi often refers to this dark phase of the practice and tries to help us understand that this part of the journey is not only necessary and valuable, but worthy of our gratitude as well:

> *If the sun wouldn't go behind*
> *The curtains at night,*
> *How would earth be illuminated in the*
>   *morning?*

The pains and challenges of the third stage, ranging from relatively mild to extremely intense, are all as natural as the pains that a woman feels during childbirth, and it helps to have the courage, strength, and commitment of a woman in labor to pass through them successfully. We all have unique patterns and ways in which we inhibit the current of the life force. When that current gets fully activated, however, it becomes a powerful force for purification, intent on dissolving whatever blocks its free passage and expression.

The second stage of the journey activates the current but the overall experience remains very pleasurable. However, as the current becomes stronger, it starts wearing away at the blockages and residues of the body and mind that ordinarily suppress its movement, and this process can hurt. In the third stage, the current may become so strong or intense that the once pleasurable feelings become very unpleasant. Like the building contractions of a woman's labor, the pains and challenges can get increasingly strong as the journey through the third stage progresses, culminating in the equivalent of the intense contractions of labor known as transition. As uncomfortable as it may be, the stage of transition always signals the imminent birth.

While it's foolish to glorify pain, it's equally foolish to protect yourself from your sensations, no matter what form they take. The dark pains and confusions of the third stage, like the recurring pains of labor that tear through a woman's belly, are the sign that the condition of union is striving to give birth to itself through you. Rumi makes this perfectly clear in this extraordinary passage from his *Discourses:*

> As long as Mary did not feel the pain of childbirth, she did not go toward the tree of blessing. Pain took her to the tree, and the barren tree bore fruit. This body is like Mary, and each of us has a Jesus inside him. If the pain appears, our Jesus will be born. If no pain arrives, Jesus will return to Origin by the same secret way he came, and we will be deprived of him and reap no joy.

The fear and shame that surround the challenges of the third stage keep most people from ever even getting close to this segment of their journey. The physical pains and distortions of the mind can be genuinely frightening; without the foreknowledge that these pains and distortions are a perfectly natural part of the process, you may feel that something is indeed wrong with you when they appear. Nothing is wrong with you.

The practice of gazing at the beloved will help you continue to navigate your way through the rings of fire that appear along the way. Rumi encourages us to accept everything that appears on our path, joys and sorrows, heaven and hell alike. He urges us to look upon ourselves as an assortment of energies, some of them light, others dark, all of them equally integral to the procession of the journey:

> *The man of heart has accepted everything.*
> *All good and bad are part of the dervish.*

He knows that you can proceed along the path only if you accept every sensation and feeling that reveal themselves, one after the next. He also knows that the sensations and feelings that we most fear or feel ashamed of are there to purify our minds and bodies and make us into ever more efficient conduits through which the waters of union can effortlessly flow.

Accept yourself, he keeps telling us. Accept everything that you are. Be impeccably honest in your relaxation, acceptance, and surrender. Don't sift through your experiences, like a doorman at a tony nightclub perusing the people lined up outside, letting in only the ones that are agreeable. The places in you that you least want to feel hoard powerful energies. By feeling into them exactly as they are, you liberate the energies and add to the net worth on the balance sheet of your heart. These energies, even the ones that are rough and frightening, represent all the many faces of God trying to give birth to themselves through you:

> This being human is a guest house.
> Every morning a new arrival,
> A joy, a depression, a meanness,
> Some momentary awareness comes
> As an unexpected visitor.
> Welcome and entertain them all.
> Even if they're a crowd of sorrows
> Who violently sweep your house
> Empty of its furniture,
> Still, treat each guest honorably.
> They may be clearing you out
> For some new delight.
>
> The dark thought, the shame, the malice,
> Meet them at the door laughing
> And invite them in.
> Be grateful for whoever comes,
> Because each has been sent
> As a guide from above.

The practice of gazing at the beloved allows you finally to feel into these rejected parts of yourself and expose them to your friend. This simple act of exposure is extremely potent in shedding the shame that ordinarily keeps these parts of yourself so well hidden. The Tibetan teachings are very clear that the forces of enlightenment that practitioners will encounter on their spiritual journey do not just have benevolent faces, but wrathful ones as well. Sometimes, these forces appear in the form of the most unimaginably gentle and peaceful energies. Other times, however, they can be truly terrifying. Both need to be accepted as they are.

Legend has it that when Padmasambhava, one of the founding fathers of Tibetan Vajrayana Buddhism, first came onto the Tibetan plateau, he found a country enslaved and tyrannized by powerful nature spirits who behaved in dark and sometimes very nasty ways. The people of the plateau were terrified of these forces and begged this newly arrived magician to destroy them once and for all. But Padmasambhava chose entirely different tactics for dealing with this problem, and his strategy is highly instructive for those of us engulfed in third-stage energies. He chose not to destroy or subdue the spirits, but rather to befriend them. He accepted them as they were, and through this gesture of true friendship, he was able to transform them into guardians and protectors of the teachings.

If you can befriend these powerful energies that live so deeply in the core of your body and mind, if you can remove the veil of shame and fear that you've thrown over them, then they will share their formidable strength with you and cease to create so much havoc in your life. But, to do this, you need to keep doing the practice. The intensity of the sensations, emotions, and states of mind that you're likely to encounter in this third stage can prompt you, once again, to avert your gaze. You may want to turn your eyes away from your friend's eyes if it becomes too challenging to face what you see in yourself.

As best you can, don't turn away. Stay looking at your friend.

Stay in the eye. His or her eyes are the only safe harbor that can make you feel secure enough to ride out the storm, to open to the extraordinarily potent energies that await you in this third stage. Through the bond of friendship that the practice forges, both you and your friend will find the strength to accept and befriend whatever sensations and states of mind may emerge. Together, you can pass through the purificatory rings of fire that lie in waiting.

Ultimately, the current that the second stage activates is stronger than your reticence about proceeding. As you continue to learn to trust in the wisdom of this current, letting it take you wherever it wants, you realize that the journey through these stages is seamless and organic. All you need to do is start from where you are and let go of any self-hating notions about where you could or should be. The first stage, in its own time, naturally takes you to the second. The second stage becomes the doorway leading into the third. If you can continue to surrender into the density and viscosity of the third stage, staying with your friend's eyes, coming right back to them when you can't help but look away, you eventually will pass through it and emerge on the other side. The long, dark night always ends. The sun always dawns in the eastern sky. The ocean comes into view. You arrive at your destination, but it is a very different "you" that sits in the raft from the person who started off so long ago.

The Sufis call this final stage of the journey *fana,* which means annihilation. The price of entering fully into this fourth stage is the giving up of your sense of separate self but, unlike the death of the physical body that awaits us all at the end of our lives, this annihilation is a birth into the life-giving waters of union itself. Just as the third stage of the journey is a more intensified version of the first stage, so is the fourth stage a higher octave of the second. The pleasures of the second stage are still, ever so subtly, appreciated by a mind that continues to perceive itself as an independent entity, separate from the world. For you to earn the pleasures of the fourth stage, however, the mind of separation needs to fall completely away and drown in the waters of union:

> *My head became drunk and passed out of itself.*
> *So my mind fell and disappeared.*

The Koran tells us that, if we want to enter into the kingdom of heaven while we're still alive on Earth, then we must die before we die. A kind of death accompanies the birthing into each successive stage of the journey. We die to who we were in order to give birth to who we're becoming. Each of these deaths can be accompanied by fear of the unknown or excitement for the adventure.

Most of us would admit that the greatest of all of our fears is the fear of death. We know that, at the moment of our death, who we've always known ourselves to be will undergo a radical and irreversible transformation. Our fear of death can be seen, however, as a projection into the future of our more immediate fear of the journey of life that we're intimately engaged in right now. Because it takes us through the successive stages of our soul, that journey always ends in the death of our separate sense of self as well.

In a strange way, then, when we say that we fear death, we're actually saying that we fear life. We fear the potency of the sensations that we can feel right now. We fear the current of the life force that, once yielded to, propels our raft down the river of our soul where our hearts become ripped open and our minds eventually dissolve. And yet, not until that happens can we bring the challenges and pains of the third stage of our journey to an end:

> *You've endured many terrible griefs*
> *But you're still under a veil—*
> *Because dying to yourself is the fundamental*
> *　principle*

And you haven't adhered to it.
Your suffering cannot end
Before this death is complete.

Once you've tasted the liberation of fana, even if for only a small moment, you become like the people who have undergone near-death experiences and who come back to the world with the powerful message that, if death is anything like what they have glimpsed, then there's nothing to fear and everything to look forward to.

The practice of gazing at the beloved will take you through all these stages, and it will take you through them over and over again. It's not a one-ticket ride. In the course of a long session of gazing at your friend, you may traverse each of these stages a multitude of times. Over an extended period of weeks, months, or even years, you may find yourself predominantly residing in one of these stages over the others.

As with all maps, the map of the four stages and the course of progression that it charts possess intrinsic limitations. Maps are guides that can help prepare us for the unusual experiences that await us as we enter into new territory and unfamiliar lands. They can never substitute, however, for the actual experiences that we encounter as we cross the frontier into that new territory. As with everything in the practice of gazing at the beloved, trust your experience above anything else. Certainly, do not try to mold or manipulate your experience so that it fits with the expectations you may have created through studying the map.

While, for some people, the progression from stage one through stage four will accurately describe their journey, for other people it won't work this way at all. Stage one can jump directly to stage three or even four, for example. Stage two can explode into stage four, momentarily bypassing the trials of stage three. A thorough immersion into the annihilation of stage four will reveal new aspects of stages one to three.

Let this presentation of the stages help you understand where you are at any given time. Let it support you to accept whatever experiences arise as you sit and gaze at your beloved friend, but don't insist that it accurately chart your actual journey. Only your soul can find its way back home. No one can tell it exactly how to do this. The goal of the practice is simply to continue surrendering to the dance, not to get to any specific place on the dance floor.

The Sufis of the Middle East could often be recognized by the patched clothing that they wore. Devoted to their practices, they rarely had much money to buy fine clothing and, instead, kept patching the holes in the few clothes they did own. Never think that the sewing of your cloak is ever complete, that the task of mending it is ever over. Just continue to pass the thread of your awareness through the eye of your partner's needle, again and yet again. Together, keep on crafting this magnificent and invisible fabric.

Do you remember Hans Christian Andersen's story about the emperor, the one who was so very fond of clothing (and whose foolishness led to an embarrassment that could be seen not just on the cheeks of his face)? If he could have only found a beloved friend with whom to dedicate himself to the creation of this fabric, then when he paraded through the streets the townspeople would have been overjoyed by the beauty that was radiating from their ruler.

Just be where you are, connect your eye to your friend's eye through the invisible thread of your shared gaze, trust in the wisdom of the practice, and allow the current of the river to take you wherever it wants. No one can ever know how long a journey they're on, so let the taking of the journey be your goal, and leave the rest to nature. All waters eventually reach the ocean. All souls eventually go home to God.

7

Laughter

One of the most common responses to the practice of gazing at the beloved is laughter. This can range from a silent smile that spreads throughout the entire body like a pandemic of happiness to the most tentative and nervous of giggles all the way to side-splitting hilarity whose loud, spluttering guffaws can cause tears to flow and the flanks of the body to ache. Everyone loves a good joke, and the practice of gazing at the beloved may be the best joke of all, a spiritual practice capable of taking people to high levels of realization while providing them with the amusement park ride of their lives.

Union makes us happy, and laughter is the most extroverted member of happiness's extended family. A little boy in a stroller, being pushed by his mother through the aisles of a department store, so fascinated by everything around him, locates your face. You see him too and feel charmed by the freshness of his being and the uninhibited joy and interest he takes in checking out everything in this new world into which he has so recently been born. Your eyes meet, and through the connection of your gaze his face erupts in a tooth-less smile and gurgling laugh that melt your heart. He's found what he was looking for, a way back to the feeling place of union that his birth into the world of separation forced him to leave behind. Some-times, even as his mother wheels him away, he'll turn in his seat and look back after you.

Later on in his childhood, he may once again explore the inti-macy of eye contact through challenging his close friends to staring contests. When schoolchildren enter into staring contests with one another, defeat is always signaled by the first outburst of laughter.

Why does the meeting of another person's gaze so often cause us to laugh? We laugh because the connection that we experience through gazing at our friend allows us to leave our familiar world behind and enter into a wholly different and quite magical one, even if only for a little minute. We laugh because we delight in the feelings and sensations of this new and unusual world. We laugh because the way in which our friend's face metamorphoses and constantly shifts its shape before our eyes makes us feel as though we had taken a hal-lucinogenic drug with a sly sense of humor and no undesirable side effects (no virtual reality game could ever be *this* good). And we laugh because we're so happy to have finally found a real friend, someone with whom we can express this deepest part of our nature, someone to whom we can show our original face, the pure and guileless inno-cence of being that existed before we had to learn to don our masks and tough it out in the world in order to lay claim to our own per-sonal bit of space and territory.

As Ida Rolf suggested, vision and sensation are intimately linked. Everything that you see registers immediately as a sensation in your body. A green light, a red light, your lover walking seductively into your bedroom, your boss storming down the hall toward your office, the blur of commuters racing to work surrounded by the endless con-crete of the city, the sun falling beneath the horizon of the ocean: all of these visual events cause different responses and activate very different sensations and feelings in your body.

If vision is touch at a distance, then the practice of gazing at the beloved can be likened to tickling at a distance. The practice awakens the sensations of your body from their long slumber, sometimes so dramatically that it feels as though your older brother had pinned you down and were tickling you until the tears flow down your face. Tickling is so effective (hence, so beloved by older siblings everywhere) because the speed with which your sensations shift from neutral to wildly overstimulated is so rapid and the new stimulation is so startling. The same is true for the practice of gazing at the beloved. You sit down with your friend, you begin gazing at each other, and almost immediately your sensations come to life as though miniature insects were break-dancing all over the surface of your body. It's a sublime tickle.

We also laugh because, somewhere deep within the genetic core of our psyche, we realize that we've pulled off a not insignificant evolutionary leap. We needn't break out cigars to congratulate ourselves, but a shared chuckle seems entirely appropriate. In the jungle of our ancestors, a lone foraging gorilla comes unexpectedly bounding out of a thicket of dense scrub growth and there, a hundred yards away across a clearing of tall grasses, spies a whole family of gorillas from an unknown tribe. The last thing that the solitary gorilla would do would be to invoke the spirit of the Rumis of the future and gaze across the clearing, attempting to establish eye contact in the hope of inviting a loving connection with this family of strangers. Were he to do that, he knows that within seconds he would have the fight of his life on his hands.

For animals whose primary impulses are territorial, the seeking out and holding of the gaze can be experienced only as an aggressive attempt to establish dominance—and this is as true in the corporate boardroom today as it was in the jungle of our forebears.

The practice of gazing at the beloved, on the other hand, has nothing at all to do with pecking orders of domination and submission. Both partners share equally in the responsibilities and rewards of the practice. Mutual gazing establishes the most intimate contact between people but, like any act of intimacy, it requires the consent of both parties. Otherwise, it is an aggressive molestation, not of the body, but of the soul of the person who doesn't feel drawn to dissolving into union with you.

In a later era, monkeys would learn to paste million-dollar smiles on their faces as a sign of goodwill if they inadvertently strayed into other monkey families' territories and wanted to get out with their fur intact. These kinds of smiles still crop up on the faces of certain politicians and game show hosts—in fact, on anybody who knows that what he or she is about to tell you isn't likely to cause you to smile in response.

The late U.S. president Lyndon Johnson was evidently a master of intimidation. He would stand about four inches from your face, gazing intently down into your eyes from above (he was a very tall man), smiling the whole time, and telling you in no uncertain terms what he wanted you to do for him. He wasn't relaxing into your gaze. He wasn't seeking a mutual surrender into the shared world of union. He was just using his physical stature and position of office to get what he wanted, cloaking everything behind a smile worthy of the bullying primates in the District of Columbia zoo.

How different, then, are the genuine smile and laugh that burst forth from practitioners who sit across from each other, holding each other's gaze, feeling themselves merging back into a single shared phenomenon:

> It is impossible to hide a smile
> In front of my beloved.

Such a smile is awarded only to friends who truly lose themselves in each other and in the practice, who so thoroughly mix their energies together that a new consciousness emerges between them. Losing yourself in this way (but finding another invaluable part of yourself through the loss) can really be very funny, and the laughter that breaks out is often a true belly laugh, engulfing the whole body in its conspiracy of divine play:

> *I laugh not just with my mouth*
> *But with my whole body*
> *Because I am completely out of myself.*

Reclaiming your birthright of union is an event worth rejoicing over. It's like getting the coat of your dreams back from God's own coatroom. What better way to rejoice than to laugh yourself silly with your friend over the good fortune of being alive together? Ultimately, we laugh best when we get the punch line, and perhaps the greatest of all jokes is that what we've been spending our lives searching for has been sitting here right under our noses (or, rather, right above our noses) the whole time.

Yes, seen from the perspective and consciousness of separation, every object and event is an island unto itself. My body is separate from yours and always will be. But through the practice of gazing at the beloved the punch line is revealed: You and I are, nonetheless, intimately bound together through our shared participation in the great ground of union, through a bond that can never ever be broken or torn apart, not by beliefs nor by any action. Just behind the world of separate appearances, penetrating it to its core, lies the domain of union in which all is one.

By exploring this other less visible world, we strike it rich, and no downturn in the market can ever take away from us what has always been ours. We may or may not become a fat cat in the world of appearances, laughing our way inanely through a succession of yachts, fancy cars, elegant parties, and ski holidays. All of us, however, are fat cats in the world of union, and the smiles across our faces, once we realize how wealthy we are, would make the Cheshire cat proud. Many cities have an exclusive Union Club where the rich and powerful congregate, but membership in that club doesn't mean much if we've forgotten about the union club to which every one of us on the planet belongs.

Many religions and spiritual paths are built primarily on bricks of tears. Others demand almost superhuman courage to climb their tall trees and pick their fruit. Still others seem just to want to scare us silly so we'll start behaving according to their dictates, our own impulses and truths be damned. But what about laughter?

Why is there no place set for Laughter at the banquet table of organized religion? Could it be that, if invited, laughter would behave so badly that it might upset first the cart bearing the golden apples (being served as the first course of temptation and enslavement), and then the whole table as well? Would Laughter have Temperance and Humility, its dinner companions seated to its right and left, lighting farts before the main course was even served? Is the high priest's chair the one place on the face of the Earth that's off-limits to a whoopee cushion? What's become of the smiling Buddhas with the roly-poly bellies and the laughing Taoists who, just before they died, concealed fireworks under their robes so that the mourners gathered at the funeral fires would be giggled, tickled, rollicked, and rolled out of their grief? Compassion is one of the most powerful and beautiful forces of human nature, but tie a smile as a wick around a glass jar of compassion, fill it with the fuel of laughter, and you have a Molotov cocktail capable of sending the blue meanies that strangle our souls racing for the exits.

Just as the practice of gazing at the beloved can shed light on the mystery surrounding the relationship between Rumi and Shams, so too can it offer clues to another enigma from within the Buddhist tradition. As the Buddha was aging and his time of death was obviously drawing near, he realized that he needed to appoint a successor, someone who would be regarded as the principal custodian for the teachings and who would be the one to be consulted if ever a controversy arose. By the time of the Buddha's death, however, there were a number of disciples who had all attained high degrees of realization. Whom should he choose to succeed him, and how should he make that choice?

One morning, the Buddha came out to give a discourse before the assembled group of monks, nuns, and lay people who were gathered to hear him, just as he had done virtually every day for the past forty years. Only, on this morning, he simply sat and looked out upon the sea of meditators sitting silently in front of him, held a flower in his hand, and didn't say a word. Many long minutes passed. Still, nothing. He kept silent. The stem of the flower twirled back and forth between his fingers. He kept scanning his eyes over the assembly as though he were looking for something. Finally, the awkward silence was broken, but not by the Buddha. One of the Buddha's most senior disciples, a monk named Mahakashyap, unable to contain himself any longer, burst out laughing. The Buddha smiled back at him and said simply, "The transmission has occurred. Mahakashyap is the next patriarch."

What had happened?! The answer to that question has proved tantalizingly elusive to Buddhist scholars ever since.

If you've ever attended a Buddhist retreat, you can probably conjure up a fair approximation of the scene that confronted the Buddha on that long-ago day. Meditation retreats provide practitioners a highly supportive environment to work seriously on their practices. Many are conducted in silence, and practitioners avoid any contact or interaction with one another. Meditators hurry into the hall and make their way to their cushions. They sit down, assume their upright posture, and begin focusing intently on the object of their practice, perhaps the passage of breath as it moves in and out of the body or the fluctuating drama of sensations and thoughts. The meditation retreat is not frivolity's primary home, nor should it be.

Sitting silently in that assembly twenty-five hundred years ago, settling into your posture, calming your mind and body through the healing power of the practice, waiting in anticipation for your beloved master to come out and speak to you, you couldn't help but be a bit startled by this inexplicable twist in the routine behavior of this teacher who never ever deviated from his daily schedule. And what was he doing, looking out over the crowd of meditators? Was he looking for someone? Had he misplaced something (this was well before car keys and reading glasses)? Hmmm . . . hope he doesn't look at me.

Perhaps, Mahakashyap was the only one in the entire assembly who wasn't unsettled by the Buddha's behavior. Perhaps, Mahakashyap kept his eyes wide open and met the Buddha's gaze directly when the Buddha looked over at him. Perhaps, Mahakashyap surrendered to the change in sensations and shift in consciousness that inevitably occurs when two people look at each other and hold each other's gaze. Perhaps, Mahakashyap found himself precipitously transported into the consciousness of union that also inevitably occurs through the linkage of eyes and vision. Certainly, when this happens to anyone for the very first time, it does feel like receiving a transmission from the other person. And then, as confirmation that this had indeed occurred, Mahakashyap—just like you and me and the little child in the stroller and the bored eighth graders in study hall—burst out laughing! And the Buddha knew he had found his man.

We need to take our practices seriously and submit to a discipline if we hope to grow the fruits that we know can ripen on the trees of spiritual teachings. Even so, we need to be on the lookout never to take ourselves too seriously and never to let ourselves go overboard in any one direction. To keep a car on the road, we constantly have to move the steering wheel back and forth, from the right to the left and back again. If we steered only to the right or to the left and never compensated in the other direction, we would end up going around in circles. So let your laughter come when it must, even if you're sitting in the most sacred temple. Then let your tears come if you find that they're queued up next. Laughter and tears, courage and fears: the path of the heart asks us to accept everything we find once we lift open our heart's lid and peer into its depths.

8

Friends and Consorts

S ometimes, beloved friends come into our lives, and we remain just that—friends. At other times, however, the currents of the practice may take us in a different direction, and we are drawn into becoming not just spiritual lovers, but sexual lovers as well. Consorts are friends in the practice with whom we have a sexual, as well as a spiritual, relationship.

Ordinarily, people expend a great deal of energy trying either to lure sex into their life or to keep it out. The practice of gazing at the beloved, however, proceeds best when there's no manipulation involved, when both participants feel completely free to surrender to the will of the current, allowing it to take them wherever it organically flows. At times, the practices will lead two people who are destined to become sexual lovers into a consensual physical embrace. The very same practice, however, will also protect those people for whom a sexual liaison is not appropriate from entering into entanglements that don't serve them. Surrender is what keeps us safe and the practice on track. If either of the friends were to impose an agenda, sexual or otherwise, onto their gazing, the train of the practice would either go off the rails or grind to a halt. Agendas are always of the mind and reflect what the mind believes it wants to make itself happy. When two people truly come together in the practice, they quickly travel beyond the mind and enter into a field of dreams where agendas have no place:

> Out beyond ideas of wrong doing and right
>   doing
> There is a field.
> I'll meet you there.

It remains my personal belief that Rumi and Shams were not sexual lovers, that the extraordinary merging that occurred between them occurred at the level of their souls only, not at the level of their bodies, and I believe there is much evidence to support this view. While Rumi's poetry is littered with references to the practice of gazing at the beloved, there is very little mention of sexual embrace at all. We know that Rumi was married twice, that both of his wives bore him children, and so we can reasonably assume that his primary orientation was heterosexual. We also know that, in hopes of keeping Shams close to him, Rumi arranged for one of the girls who had been brought up in his house to be married to Shams and that Shams loved this girl deeply. Later in his life, he would enter again into the practice of gazing at the beloved with two more great friends, both of whom were also male. These two relationships were much more public and well documented than his relationship with Shams, and there has never been any suggestion or evidence that these relationships were at all sexual.

Viewing the relationship between Rumi and Shams in a nonsexual light has nothing to do with gender politics, as same-sex lovers can enter into the full range of this practice every bit as deeply and successfully as heterosexual lovers. What it valuably shows us is that the practice can take two beloved friends into the most lovingly intimate merging and embrace of the soul without there ever being any kind of physical contact whatsoever between them.

However, just as vision is capable of stimulating sensation from a distance, so also can direct physical contact between one body and another support two lovers in seeing deeply into each other's soul. So, for the purposes of this chapter, let's leave Rumi and Shams, these two greatest exemplars of the nonsexual side of the practice of gazing at the beloved, and travel both eastward and backward in time to the high Tibetan plateau. There, the primordial Buddha called Samantabhadra sits naked, cross-legged in meditation on a lotus throne, while his female counterpart, Samantabhadri, equally naked, sits astride him in passionate embrace, her eyes connected to his eyes, her lips and tongue dancing with his lips and tongue, her breasts pressed into his chest, her legs wrapped around his waist, stabilized and secured in the posture by his penis, which is inserted deep into the wet folds of her vagina. These two great lovers are clearly not actors in a Hollywood film who fake their thrusts and pulls, their moans and sighs. No, they are a truly divine couple who use their sexual bonding to transport them to the highest spiritual station. Let these two become our guides for those times when we might enter into the practice with a beloved friend and feel the urgency to join not just our souls, but our bodies as well.

The goals of sexual play and spiritual discipline have commonly been presented as incompatible with each other. Indeed, the overpowering strength of sexual longing has forever teased, tormented, and challenged spiritual practitioners who view that longing as a hindrance rather than a help in their work. Renunciative forms of spiritual practice have traditionally encouraged their practitioners to leave behind the comforts of companionship and the joys of this world to seek something supposedly greater or more noble. While such renunciation works well for some people, for a great many others it's simply a tragedy. Samantabhadra and Samantabhadri offer the good news that there is another way, that sexual play is not necessarily inimical to spiritual passion but can support and reinforce it. Sex does not have to throw water on the fires of enlightenment but can fuel its blaze instead. It all depends on how we approach our sexuality.

Much of the problem with modern sexuality is that lovers can become so exclusively focused on the feelings and sensations in their own genitals that they lose awareness of the rest of their body and of the soul of the one they're embracing. The motivation behind the sex, then, becomes personal gratification rather than the mutual dissolving into a shared awareness of union, a meeting and mating of souls. No pleasure, however sublime it may be, is ultimately capable of satisfying anyone if it falls short of taking both lovers to union.

From the beginnings of time, Samantabhadra and Samantabhadri have been demonstrating the way to resolve this problem. Enjoy the bliss of surrendering to the powerful energies of the body, they tell us, but don't lose yourself in these feelings. Instead, maintain presence as you enter or are entered by your beloved. Maintain presence the whole time you're engaged. Join bliss (Saman-tabhadri) with presence (Samantabhadra). In this way, the joy and pleasure of coupling with your beloved can take you directly into the union that you both seek, rather than leave you feeling further alienated from it.

Samantabhadra and Samantabhadri's instructions for accomplishing this are clear for anyone to see. We often close our eyes in lovemaking, and lose ourselves in the flushed haze of our genital bliss. Not these two. They have their eyes wide open, and they're looking directly at each other. They penetrate each other with more than the energy of their genitals; they move in and out of each other with the energy of their souls through the shared connection of their gaze. That's the first thing they're telling us about sacred sex: maintain contact with your lover through the gaze. Make love with your souls as well as your bodies.

Because the practice of gazing at the beloved powerfully stimulates the feeling-presence of the entire body, what Samantabhadra
and Samantabhadri are also telling us indirectly is to make love not
just with our genitals but with every single cell of our joined bodies. In the intensity of sexual embrace, consorts can more easily feel
every little cell and sensation in their bodies. Our passionate Buddhas tell us to take advantage of the strength of love's energies. The
bliss of those full-bodied energies creates a powerful vortex capable
of drawing us into a union far greater than the union we feel if we
remain fixated on the sensations in our genitals alone.

Through stimulating the eye center, the practice also powerfully
activates our sense of presence, for it's just behind the eyes that we
feel our presence—that feeling of "I exist" and "I am here"—the
most strongly. By holding each other's gaze, Samantabhadra and
Samantabhadri teach us to stay present in the middle of our dance of
passion. They remind us that only when bliss and presence are joined
together in concert can we find our way back to union; if they're not
so joined, then we may still feel unfulfilled.

In many Buddhist and Christian practices, for example, a great
deal of attention is paid to the workings of the mind and the creation
of mindful presence, but the feelings and sensations of the body and
the natural universe of pleasure may become overlooked, blocked, or
devalued in comparison. The result can be clarity without energy, presence without bliss. Conversely, in some yogic or devotional practices
the energies of the body can be profoundly activated and explored
with much less attention paid to understanding the workings of the
mind; in these cases, practitioners can tend to get lost in their sensations and feelings. The result here is energy without clarity.

Samantabhadra and Samantabhadri demonstrate that we need to
do both, that we need to combine the roots of our ancestral energies
that are still very alive and well in our bodies (even though we have
largely relegated them to hibernation) with the growth of conscious-

ness that has accompanied our mental evolution. One without the other just isn't capable of delivering what we're truly longing for. When we hold the gaze of the other, whether we're sitting across from our beloved friend or holding his or her naked body close to our own, we activate both the energies of the body and the presence of the mind.

In many ways, consciousness and even the physical body itself can be viewed as electrical phenomena. Positively and negatively charged energies are constantly colliding and interacting with each other on subatomic levels, and their friction gives rise to consciousness and matter alike. One of electricity's favorite mediums of conduction is water. Therefore, Samantabhadra and Samantabhadri instruct us to join together the watery centers of the body to facilitate and promote the energetic linkage that occurs in the practice. The eyes are always watery; the tongue and mouth, even more so. The juices of the woman's vagina help her receive the man's erect penis. In addition to the stimulation of these three major centers of bodily moisture, if the whole body can then become thoroughly bathed in sweat from the sexual exertion, so much the better.

So gaze at your lover while you're making love. Let your tongues and mouths dance together to help ground the powerful energies that the gaze activates. And then surrender totally. Let the intensity of this sacred sex take you both straight to God. As you join pelvis-to-pelvis, mouth-to-mouth, and eye-to-eye, your hearts will open as one.

The true purpose of relationship, beyond fulfilling the urge to procreate, is to come home to God, and the widespread failure of relationship can be directly attributed to the fact that so few of us really want to do that. Most of us enter into relationship for security, comfort, possession; the direct experience of God, however, has nothing to do with any of these things. Instead of security or stability, the Sufi experiences a world of constant, shimmering change. Instead of grasping at the relative joys and comforts associated with most relationships, the Sufi willingly opens to a birthing process, undergoing an often painful labor in order to birth into union with God, the true source of comfort. The Sufi doesn't possess his or her beloved friend but dissolves with the other into a shared participation of union.

So, men, worship your woman as though she were a goddess visiting this Earth. She is. Women, surrender to your energy (it's what your man wants), and then open to your lover. Receive him. Let him pour his energy fully into you, into every cell of your body and corner of your mind (isn't that what you want?).

When two people sit silently on opposite ends of a sofa, the energies stimulated through the holding of the gaze are formidable enough. Add to this the powerful feelings of sexual excitement, and you have a potent brew indeed. The great promise of consort relationships is that the sexual energies can powerfully catalyze the work of dissolving together back into the ground of union. The caveat of consort relationships is that the practitioners must contend with and surrender to even stronger energies. If these energies become blocked in any way, if one or both of the consorts are unable or unwilling to surrender to them totally, then the train of the practice will become stalled and the passion in the relationship may peter out. Most people enter into a love relationship as consorts, but are quickly tested as to their willingness and ability to surrender to a love that is beyond love.

If your great friend becomes your sexual lover, then sit with each other for long hours, connecting deeply through the gaze, before you join your bodies together. If you do this, it will dramatically deepen the quality of your love play. Women, come more. Men, ejaculate less. Men, serve your women. Honor their willingness to allow you to enter them by continually spreading the energies that build in your genitals throughout your entire body. When you feel yourself close to coming, slow down your thrusting, relax your body completely, and then surrender to a long inhalation that fills your entire body from head to foot. In this way, you will forego your ejaculation (but not your orgasmic bliss) and be able to ride wave after wave after wave of energy with her. Surf's up! Can you really imagine a dedicated surfer riding just one wave and then paddling back to the beach to call it a day?

Let the woman's orgasms fill you both. She can come and still want to play more. If the man ejaculates, your lovemaking will come to an end. As you learn to play together in this way, your sex will naturally come to a resting place that signals that it's time for the man to withdraw his penis from his beloved's vagina. Then, lie on your sides together, facing each other, and connect again through the eyes. The depths of the practice that are touched during these moments reveal a gift that is greater than the temporary pleasures of ejaculation.

Ejaculation has been man's sacred entitlement ever since organic life emerged out of the ooze and discovered that its chances for survival would best be served by splitting itself into two sexes whose longing for their lost half would result in the constant urgency to procreate. As long as procreation for survival was the point, man's ejaculation was not just an entitlement, but a responsibility as well. But if the purpose of sex isn't to create new life but rather to drown with one's lover in the waters of union, then ejaculation becomes neither entitlement (man dominating woman) nor responsibility (man serving woman), but, well, more of a minor gaffe than anything else. ("Oops. Sorry about that, hon. But no worries. We're getting closer to getting this down.") Modern man may like to ejaculate, but he doesn't want to impregnate, and just maybe this is one of those instances when it truly is appropriate to throw out both the bath water and the baby.

Man's fixation on ejaculation as the goal of sex also selfishly overlooks the physiological fact that women are wired to want orgasms every bit as much as are men. From the point of view of procreation, however, this craving in women serves little purpose other than providing a motivation, like the carrot dangled in front of the donkey, for her to want sex as much as the man. And, if you truly listen to woman's widespread and understandable dissatisfaction with the "joy" of procreative sex (whose biological purpose is best served by the man's ejaculating as quickly as possible), she may attain her orgasm about as often as the donkey attains the carrot. But from the point of view of what might be called *creational sex,* whose goal and purpose is for both the man and the woman to merge, for a brief and glorious moment, back into the consciousness of union out of which God created the heavens and the Earth, then woman's orgasms are not only as important as man's, but even more so.

If you and your lover, like Samantabhadra and Samantabhadri, are truly sincere about drowning together in the waters of union, then you need to swim far out beyond the shoreline of procreative sex, out into the deepest waters, and then just drop and drop and keep on dropping, ever and always deeper. A man's ejaculation is like the activation of an inflatable device that will pull you both right back up to the surface. A woman's orgasms keep you sinking deeper.

We may live in a world in which fast food has become the norm, but the task of merging back into union can't be rushed. You need to simmer your ingredients slowly, over time, but never for a moment let the passion and heat of your fire go out. It's a bit like keeping a pot of soup just at the edge of a boil but never letting it erupt and spill out in a mess over the stove and counter.

Can any man honestly look at the image of Samantabhadra and Samantabhadri making passionate love for all of us down through eternity and really believe that his divine entitlement is just to come and come and come some more? Any man knows that, were he to do that, there would be little chance that he could manage to remain upright in body and erect in penis for very long at all. And can any man honestly believe that, no matter how cool a stud, famous a rock star, or financially secure a billionaire he might be, a truly great and glorious woman would be content just to sit on him down through the ages while he did his business with her if she were not getting the greatest pleasure from their love play, over and over again?

In the beginning, as you and your lover explore the practices of Samantabhadra and Samantabhadri, you will need to work together in close communication so that the man can learn to bypass his ejaculatory reflex, spreading and circulating its orgasmic energies throughout his entire body, every cell of it, prolonging the descent into union rather than going over the top, spurting his gush of ejaculate, and effectively bringing everything to an end. New joys await you both, and the greatest of all joys is union.

As with everything else about the practice of gazing at the beloved, there are no ultimately right or wrong ways of doing the practice in the context of lovemaking. In the beginning, both lovers will want to work consciously to help the man overcome his mechanical attachment to ejaculation. Once the man has learned how natural and easy it is not to come, once he has developed enough ability to ride his woman's orgasms all the way to their completion without having to bail out before she gets there, then you both can continue to surrender to the practice, allowing it once again to take you wherever it wants.

Men, if you have been getting increasingly nervous while reading this chapter, fret not. There will be times when you and your lover will surrender to ever deeper energies and embraces that naturally lead to your coming together, and even the most accomplished tantric masters tell us that occasional ejaculation is healthy, but you will no longer have to ejaculate every time you enter your lover like a programmed procreative robot. Your lover will love you for it. And you will love yourself as well.

All this talk of esoteric sex notwithstanding, what is most important is that you trust and honor the karmic currents that have brought you together. One or both of you may not be free to explore all the possibilities that the practice of gazing at the beloved has to offer. Other obligations may limit the intensity of your communion, or you may have relationships with others whose sanctity you don't wish to violate or threaten. If that's so, accept it, and explore the practices with your friend within guidelines to which you both agree. Know that it's not necessarily better or worse for your great friend also to be your lover. It's just different, with its own advantages and disadvantages.

In my life, I've been fortunate to have had a number of great friends in the practice. My first friend was a much older man, and our relationship was not sexual. My next friend was a fiery and beautiful woman, and our relationship was very sexual. My next great friend was also a wonderful, deep woman, but our relationship was never sexual. What was always far more important than whether or not we became sexual lovers was whether or not we became fully engaged in the practice. So, engage your great friend, and then let the energies of this engagement be your guide as you're pulled downward to drown together in the waters of union.

Even though the model of Samantabhadra and Samantabhadri is a heterosexual one, this doesn't mean that same-sex lovers cannot equally participate in this practice. Female couples can mix their vaginal fluids through their genital contact and embrace. All homosexual lovers can kiss and, most important, they can gaze at each other during their love play every bit as powerfully and effectively as their heterosexual counterparts. All lovers—gay and straight, man-to-man, man-to-woman, woman-to-woman—who like to caress and hold and even enter their lover from behind may wish to place a large mirror at the head of their bed. Whenever their sexual posture makes it difficult for them to look at each other directly, they can still share their gaze through the mirror.

And do not think that these teachings about sexuality apply only to two friends who meet each other and enter together into the practice of gazing. They apply equally to already established lovers who discover the gazing practice and choose to explore it together. If you already are connected to a lover—be it a brand new relationship or a marriage of twenty years—invite the gazing practice into your relationship. Make your lover your great friend in the practice as well, and your relationship will be transformed.

Whether you entwine your body with another or not, become a lover. That's Rumi's and Shams's message to us, and it's Samantabhadra's and Samantabhadri's as well. Whether or not you become sexual lovers, entwine your soul with your lover's soul. Once you establish that connection, then rejoice in it, and surrender to its pulls and pushes, its pulsing thrusts and withdrawals. The linkage of two souls forms a perfect wave on which the two great friends can surf in tandem. Ride this wave all the way in to the shore. Paddle back out, catch the next wave, and do this over and over again.

Know that there's no shame in falling off a wave. Just learn how to take your falls as gracefully as possible, and then get back up on your board together. Let your relationship with your friend or consort be as deeply surrendered to these powerful currents as your systems can handle. Stay in the gaze. Stay in the swirling pool of sensations. Stay present. Play with each other in this way as much as you possibly can.

Women, by honoring your man as a god, you evoke the goddess within you. Men, treat your woman as an expression of the divine, and you will become that too. Only in this way can men and women become partners in peace and make gender wars a thing of the past. If you do this, your relationship will become a sacred thing, a vehicle that can take you both to the Divine—and isn't that what you want beyond anything? Then you and your beloved will be able to sing to each other, in the words of Suzin Green, a contemporary bard and lover of the great energies of the ground of union:

I have seen the light
Oh, when it's shining.
I have been blinded by the light
From your eyes.

I have held on to you
All through the day,
All through the night,
Into the morning.

I sing praises to you.
I sing praises to you.
I sing praises to you.

And know that it doesn't matter if you hold on to your friend's body and soul, or his or her soul alone. What does matter is for you to hold on to your beloved and for your beloved to hold on to you through the shared connection of your gaze. Hold on to that connection, and let it guide you in your journey. Whether you physically touch or not, embrace each other through the gaze, and enjoy the feeling of two souls becoming one.

PART III

Alone Together

"Here's lookin' at you, kid."
Rick Blaine, in happier days,
from *Casablanca*

9

Learning to See

We began this book with a simple question: where do we look to find the face of God? The simplest answer is that God's face is everywhere, but in order for it to appear, we need to learn how to see. Ordinarily, the objects in our visual field speak to us of separation. They are so *out there* and we are so *in here;* the gulf between them and us appears unbridgeable. Because our conventional perception of the world reinforces our belief in separation, seekers after God have commonly assumed that the world of appearances is a veil that separates us from God and that God must reside beyond the world of form altogether. For the most part, however, that assumption has not proved a happy one. A happier way to heal the separation is to realize that *out there* and *in here* are not so very far apart after all. If the objects in our visual field could begin to speak to us of union instead of separation, then the seeker after God would not have to leap beyond the world but could swim in it instead.

The easiest way to heal the misperception that the world of

appearances separates you from God is to put all your visual attention onto a single object and gaze at it raptly. Simply look, relax the body completely, and over time you and that object will merge into a single phenomenon. Where a moment before there was separation, now there is union. While any object will work for this exercise, it helps if the object you choose is one that you dearly love—and what better object could there possibly be than the face of your beloved friend? Through the practice of gazing at the beloved, *out there* and *in here* become one:

> If you want to know God,
> Then turn your face toward your friend,
> And don't look away.

But, realistically, you cannot look at your friend forever. A time will come when you each need to leave the other and tend to your family or your business or the simple care of your body. Spiritual practices are never an end in themselves; they serve, rather, as a means to living more happily in the world. So, when we leave our practices behind, we shouldn't have to leave behind the awarenesses that they've revealed to us. When we can no longer see the face of our beloved friend, we should still be able to take the feeling of union with us as we move back out into the world. "Wherever you turn, there is the face of God," says the Koran.

How can we learn to look out upon the multitude of objects of the world, the many different features of God's one face, and still maintain the awareness of union that we feel so strongly when we're gazing into the face of our beloved friend? What have we learned from the practice that we can apply to all of our seeing? How can we continue with the practice when we move away from our beloved friend and find ourselves once again alone?

The first thing that you can do is to extend the practice to include the objects of nature. Go into the forest and gaze at a tree. Go into the mountains and gaze at a sheer rock face. Go to the top of a high hill or to the edge of a lake or an ocean and gaze up at the sky and out into distant space. Just as you gaze at your beloved friend, gaze at an object of nature and melt the energies of your body with the energies that you feel in that object. Merge with the tree, the rock face, or the sky just as you merge with your friend. When nature is really seen, it releases its healing energies to the perceiver, and through that healed perception the truth of union comes into view.

Much of our contemporary malaise can be directly attributed to the loss of our connection with nature. By losing touch with the energies and sensations inside our bodies, we've severed our connection to the greater world of nature of which we're so intimately a part. The domain of union that spiritual seekers strive to contact is not some kind of exotic or esoteric condition. It is our simplest and most natural state; but we need to be here, fully in our bodies, and we need to heal our alienation from nature, both within and without, in order to experience it.

When you walk outside into nature, open yourself to the trees and the grasses and the rocks and the flowers, the warm sunshine, the cold rain, the winds, the animals. Feel their presence just as you feel the presence of your great friend when you gaze at him or her. The more you relax into that presence, the more you will realize that you are inextricably a part of it. By reestablishing your inherent connection to nature, you regain your participation in the world of union.

No matter how profound your inner searching and reflection might be, you are someday going to have to come out of yourself and rejoin the energies of your body and mind with the larger energies of nature. Wilhelm Reich, a student of Freud's who broke away from his teacher to explore how the energies of the body affect the health of the mind, believed that truth could be known only through reestablishing our intimate connection with the larger energies of the world outside ourselves: "Truth is immediate, full contact between life that perceives and life that is being perceived."

It used to be that most people lived in the country and were on intimate terms with the cycles of the seasons and the energies of the Earth, but not any more. Urban dwellers may look upon trees as a kind of oddity and ground that is not paved as menacing. If you lose touch with the natural world, then the individual objects of nature begin to appear hard and impenetrable, a kind of alien presence. If you can commune with them through your gaze, however, this perception starts to soften right before your eyes.

Objects look opaque or dull only when you withhold your energy from merging with theirs. This holding quality distorts your perception in much the same way that, when you put dark glasses on, everything that you look at becomes dark. When you quit holding back on your energy, however, it naturally radiates outward and recombines with all that it's separated itself from. When this happens, everything that you see begins to soften and shimmer.

Just as your energies naturally wanted to merge with the energies of your beloved friend, so too do they want to merge with the energies of nature. Just as you and your beloved friend become beautiful and vibratory to each other when you're deeply dissolved in your shared gaze, so too does nature become truly beautiful and luminous when you open your energies to hers. And don't think it's just a one-way street. Nature will love you for your generosity as well.

Walk through nature with your eyes wide open. Run through nature, surrendering to the energies that surge through your body, joining them with the glorious energies of our world through your vision. (Remember, vision is touch at a distance.) Better yet, dance through nature. That's what Rumi did. Relax your body, surrender to the current that moves everything, and let yourself become a conduit for your own deep energies. Let them dance through you however they want to, uncontrolled and spontaneous. Let Nature be your dance partner. Follow her lead; she'll show you the way. Only if you resist her might you step on her foot. Dance with her until you become one with her. Nature's energies are welcoming. They're always calling you to come back home to them.

After some time, when you feel ready, walk back into town, right into the middle of it, the scurry and hurry, the hard man-made structures made from hard man-made materials (glass, steel, and concrete), the neon lights, the ugly glare, the pleasant parks, the artificial entertainments that can't really dispel the silent bafflement and desperation, the basic goodness of the people that even the desperation can't conceal. You can see it all. The modern cityscape can be a harsh environment. Its sights can assault your eyes. Its sounds can assail your ears. Its pollution can hurt your body.

But still, even here, wherever you look is the face of God. By paying attention to the sensory reality—the sounds, sights, sensations, smells, and tastes—you remain present. Whatever you look upon, see it as God's face. Whatever you hear, hear it as God's voice. Whatever you feel, feel it as God's touch. Take it all in, its full spectrum of appearances, its dreariness as well as its resplendence, its faded hues as well as its rich tones, its dust as well as its water. Open yourself to it as best you can. Presence is the key that opens divinity's door. If you knew that you were looking at the face of God right now, wouldn't you surrender to that vision completely?

When you're out in the world, away from your beloved friend, become seeing. Let go of thinking that the goal of the practice is to see something special, a vision perhaps, or to become something extraordinary, a seer or a visionary. Self-aggrandizements of any kind puff us up too much so that we can't slip through the narrow crack that leads to union's domain. Just become the simple act of seeing. Whenever your eyes are open, vision is there. So just keep looking. If your eyes are open but you're not registering what you see in front of them, you enter again into separation:

Whenever you stop looking
Struggle appears.
Wherever you look
Pleasure, drunkenness, and rejoicing show their
    face.

God's face may have the complexion of a newborn, or it may be covered over with warts, but it will always make you stagger and rejoice in the pleasures of union. If you become seeing, the whole world that you look out upon will take on the shape of God's face. The way to become seeing is to see not just with your two physical eyes, but with every cell of your body. Isn't this how you've learned to look at your beloved friend?

You don't see from your physical eyes. They're only your apertures of vision. Take a look inside, and locate the place from which you truly see. In your most relaxed and open state, you'll find that it's below and quite a ways behind your physical eyes. When you begin to pay attention to this place, you'll further discover that you can contact it the most clearly only when you relax your entire body and feel it as a unified field of tactile sensations. When you feel your body in this way and look out onto whatever is in front of you, you realize that your entire body is your organ of vision. See with your entire body. Merge your awareness of your body as a unified field of sensations with the greater field of vision that you look out onto:

Dissolve your whole body into Vision.
Become seeing, seeing, seeing!

Merge your seeing with what you see. If you do this, you will shatter the fiction of *out there* and *in here*. Seeing and seen will come together as one phenomenon. In addition to offering graphic teachings on the right relations between men and women, Samantabhadra and Samantabhadri also symbolically represent the concepts of seeing and seen: Samantabhadra is the mirrorlike energy of pure awareness, and Samantabhadri represents the objects that awareness perceives. Join those two together in a perceptual copulation.

Try it right now. Put this book down for a moment, and let your eyes move around the room. Don't look at anything in particular. Just see whatever's in front of you. Feel the place *in here* from which you see. Be aware of the objects *out there* that you're seeing. Then, feel how these two aspects of existence love and embrace each other. Like Samantabhadra and Samantabhadri, they're making love for all eternity.

Acknowledge that the place from which you see and what you see are always joined together. It can't be otherwise. Seeing and seen are very relentless lovers. They never seem to tire of each other, nor are they capable of taking a break. As long as you're going to be making visual love all of your life, let your seeing be joyous and rich.

Spiritual teachings tell us that the mind is to become clear, like a mirror that reflects whatever is set before it without preference or prejudice. Take these instructions literally. Let your mind become a mirror, engaged in the clear perception of seeing. When the visual field is completely present to you, the mind will be clear, calm, and very empty. Involuntary thoughts (and the physical tensions that support them) will drop away, just like dust that's wiped clean from the surface of a mirror. Can a mirror ever be separated from the objects that are reflected on its surface?

Become mirroring. Relax the tension in your eyes. For the mind to function as a pure mirror the two eyes need to merge their stereoscopic perception into a single vision, and they can do this only through relaxing completely. Let go of seeing with your two eyes and practice seeing with your single mirror of vision.

Whatever's in front of you, whether you like it or not, see it. That's how a mirror behaves. It doesn't search out some things and reject others. When you look selectively, according to the biases and agendas of the mind, you create tension around your eyes, and you're drawn back into seeing from the physical eyes themselves. Relax your eyes. Relax the whole body. Then, open to vision. Let your two eyes see as one, and feel how deeply relaxed your body becomes. This is what Jesus meant when he said, "Let thine eye be single, and thy whole body will be filled with light."

If you can learn to see with your whole body, feeling the natural merging that occurs between the action of vision and its objects, then the small crack between the two worlds will open into a thoroughfare, and you will realize a great secret: *out there* and *in here* occupy the same space. From the perspective of separation, such a perception is ridiculous, but from the perspective of union, it's how things are. Both perspectives are equally valid. One isn't necessarily any more ultimately correct than the other. They simply reflect the bias of the perceiver. By healing the estrangement and isolation of the perspective of separation, however, the perspective of union can significantly lessen the human condition of suffering. To regain the birthright of union is our greatest human joy. Which perspective do you want for yourself?

To make this perspective and way of being in the world more vivid, apply the lessons that you've learned from gazing at your beloved friend to your movements through life. Experience your whole body all at once as a unified field of tactile sensations, and see the entire visual field in front of your eyes as a unified field as well. Let go of focusing on any single object in that field, like a hawk searching for its dinner in the grassy fields below, and see the entire visual field all at once. Relax your gaze as much as you can. Pay as much attention to the peripheries of your roughly elliptical visual field as you do to the objects at the center of that field.

Remember the principle of ma zagha, of looking with eyes that don't roam. When you're able to see the visual field all at once, as a unified phenomenon, your eyes don't need to dart around so much, the way they do when you're dreaming. From the perspective of separation, union may seem like some kind of dream; but you can come out of the dream of separation and enter into the reality of union when you keep your eyes and gaze relaxed.

It's so easy to dissolve into union when you're sitting in the presence of your beloved friend for long, unbroken hours. It's much more difficult to maintain that blessed condition when you're moving about in the world. When you're with your friend, the process of thought falls away naturally; but when you're out in the world it tugs at you constantly with its inane pronouncements, pulling you out of the present moment back into its stories about the past and future. When you become lost in thought, you forfeit the awareness of your whole body as a unified field of sensations and retreat into the small space of your head. Where a moment earlier your energy was evenly distributed through your entire body, now it all becomes lodged in the overcrowded quarters of your cranium, right behind your eyes, as though the rest of your body didn't even exist. When a man feels too much tension building in his genitals during lovemaking, he needs to relax and redistribute the energy throughout his entire body if he doesn't want to erupt in ejaculation. When you feel too much tension gathering in your eyes or your head, recognize it as a sign that you need to relax and distribute the energy more evenly again throughout your body. Otherwise, you might wander off in involuntary thought and lose the single mirror of vision that allows you to remain in union.

Wherever you look, God is there. Can you see the face of the Divine? It's not hiding behind anything. It's right there in front of you, as plain as day, where it's always been. A monk once asked the Zen master Joshu, "What is the word of the ancients?" The term *the word of the ancients* was used to describe the ultimate mystery that the tradition of Zen has so elegantly and industriously probed. Joshu was silent for a moment and then replied, "Listen carefully! Listen carefully!" If someone asks you where to find the face of God, you could answer in much the same way: "Look carefully! Look carefully!" If you look carefully you will see that, everywhere you look, God is there looking back at you.

Vision is our dominant sense, the sensory modality to which we accord our greatest trust and allegiance. Seeing is believing. Even so, extend your seeing to include your other senses as well. Let your mirroring be multisensorial: See what's in front of you right now. Hear the sounds that are here to be heard right now. Feel the sensations that are coursing through your body right now. The face of God shows itself not just through the sights of the world, but through the sounds, the bodily sensations, the smells and tastes as well.

When you move away from your beloved friend and venture back out into the world alone, know that you never leave him or her behind completely, but that you will always take the bond you both share with you. Rumi saw this connection, once forged, as absolute:

We are always and ever in communication with that person with whom we are in union—in silence, in his presence, and even in his absence.

And remember this simple phrase that will keep you safe no matter what you encounter, no matter what crosses your path: *Stop, look, and listen.* It worked for you when you first learned how to cross a crowded street. Let it work for you again as you cross over from separation into union. Whenever you're out in the world and get caught up in the mad pace of life, whenever you're feeling overwhelmed by the incessant stimuli of sensory objects and thoughts that are constantly bombarding you, wrestling with one another for your attention, just stop. Slow down. Take a moment. Feel your body. Only when you feel every little bit of it can you truly move freely, as a free man or a free woman. Look. See everything as the face of God. And listen. Hear God's voice speaking to you and to everybody else who has the ears to hear. If you stop, look, and listen, you will always be safe, and union will applaud your safe crossing from separation's corner over to its own.

10

Heartbreak

*T*here are only two events powerful enough to shatter the protective casing that ordinarily surrounds the heart and keeps its life-giving energies contained. The first is to fall in love, to meet someone whose existence so thrills you that you get torn open by feelings and joys that you never knew before. The second is to have your heart broken, to lose the love that was sustenance to your soul and to be left behind, discarded, desolate, and devastated. On the path of love, both are apparently necessary. Both happened to Rumi. Both have happened to me. Haven't they happened to you?

The fear of the second event is so strong that it scares off many people from ever even opening to the possibilities of the first. We all love the feeling of falling in love; we all hate how closely the fear of losing that love follows on the heels of love's arrival. Some of us will craft contracts and swear to agreements in our attempt to keep the pain of loss and heartache at bay. Even so, we know that fending off heartache is futile and that all relationships are going to end. One of the partners is going to leave the other or die, and no contract or agreement can ever prevent this. Once the dance of love begins, the only thing that we can know for sure is that somehow, in some way, our heart is going to get ripped open. This tearing may be ecstatic or it may be devastating; it may even be both, but it's going to happen.

Meeting a friend and falling in love is always risky business. We may be transported to heights previously unknown and witness sights previously unseen. But on a tightrope stretched so high above the Earth, there's also the chance that we might stumble. A fall from such a height is going to hurt, and won't involve just minor scrapes and bruises. When we're deserted by a lover, someone with whom we were just a day before so intimately bonded and mixed, the pain we feel is as intense as the happiness we've lost.

While Shams's sudden appearance in Rumi's life twice unleashed the greatest of ecstasies in the young teacher, his departure twice provoked an equally intense torment. While Rumi's poems that most of us have heard speak of the beauty and bliss of being wildly drunk on love's wine, there are just as many others in which he cries out in bitterness and heartache, his bottle empty and broken, his whole being a suddenly rudderless boat set cruelly adrift on the tides of despair:

> *Your cruel separation*
> *Is driving me completely crazy!*

The path of love is not for the weak of heart, and yet even the strongest and most courageous among us will have our hearts shattered into a thousand pieces when the beloved leaves us or passes beyond this world. For this final shattering, this expulsion from the Garden of Eden, is as much a part of the path of love as are the joys of the initial entrance and meeting. It opens up feelings of the heart that rarely emerge when we're newly in love.

Ultimately, the entire range of feelings and sensations in the heart need to be felt, surrendered to, and integrated. At some point, we will be alone again, but if we've managed to traverse the joys and pains of the heart with any kind of grace, it won't be the same kind of aloneness that we felt before our beloved friend came into our life. After having been in love, even if for only a little while, we can never again be quite the same.

From the earliest poems and letters, two things become clear. The first is that Rumi virtually deified Shams and regarded Shams with awe as the source of his awakening:

> Your eyes every moment
> Open thousands of eyes and offer thousands of
>   sights.
> God gave you the same force and power He
>   gave to Jesus.
> It was you who taught my eyes how to see,
> And my eyes look back at you now in awe and
>   admiration,
> Wondering how this could have possibly
>   happened.

The second is that he viewed Shams's departure as a callous rending of the bond of love that the two had forged together; an incomprehensible running away from the sacred love that both men valued above everything; a truly cruel gesture designed to throw him into the dark night of despair. Like all jilted lovers, Rumi was not above resorting to blame and accusation in his attempts to convince Shams to return:

> For lovers, to run away from the beloved
> Is a hundred times more
> Blasphemous than blasphemy.

But like all jilted lovers, he eventually found that whining and heaping on guilt never succeed in changing the beloved's mind and bringing him or her back. It just makes things worse.

From Rumi's perspective, Shams's decision to leave Konya violated all common sense. But Shams's perspective may have been quite different; perhaps there was some method to his madness after all, some deeper design behind what may first appear to have been an impetuous and childish reaction. Perhaps he saw that his young friend had placed him on too high a pedestal, that Rumi's veneration of Shams and his attachment to Shams as the source of his awakening were standing in the way of Rumi's greater destiny. The true source and seed of our awakening can be found only in our very own heart, never in someone else's. Another can assist in the process of our awakening, helping to warm that seed until it germinates, takes root, and blossoms, but ultimately we are the only soil in which true awakening can occur.

If Rumi was losing sight of the truth that we are all equal before God, then what could Shams possibly do to help his beloved friend but leave him so that he would be forced to wrestle with his soul and eventually come to realize the error of his perception? And perhaps Shams also sensed that Rumi needed to confront some powerful feelings and sensations that could not come to the surface so long as he was immersed in the euphoria of union. Later, after the horrible passage of heartbreak, Rumi would come to understand that Shams's departures were a necessary component in Rumi's ownership of his awakening; that the process of wrestling with his soul and traversing the torments of separation was also a necessary leg of the journey; that love is not just a dreamy delight:

> *Love is not the business of delicate people*
> *Who fall asleep at the gathering.*
> *Love is for brave ones, for wrestlers, o son.*

Still later in his life, after he had integrated the lessons of his time with Shams, Rumi would understand that the recipe for opening the heart depends on bliss and heartache in equal measure:

> *The body that drank this wine,*
> *The heart that became drunk with this wine,*
> *Will mature by cooking in the fire of separation.*

> *I am adding the water of cruelty to the honey*
> *   of ecstasy*
> *Because you can't eat pure honey all by itself.*
> *It's just too sweet to go down your throat.*

The loss of the beloved can cause great shock to the system, and yet the awful feeling of that rending reveals a whole other layer of sensations that the practitioner on the path of love needs to open up to. These deeper sensations are ingredients as necessary in the baking of the bread of love as are the first sensations of happiness that the initial meeting pours into the pan.

The walker on the path of love needs to traverse all the feelings of the heart. It's not just about the light of bliss and ecstasy. The shadows of sorrow, despair, jealousy, and doubt are necessary components of the path as well, and just as we soar when our hearts fly open, so too do we suffer when they're shot from the sky. On the path of love the heart is eventually going to be broken open so that the energies that lie therein can expand and evolve into a whole new dimension. The immense pain of the heart then becomes the next doorway through which we must pass as we continue on in our journey. Trying to protect the heart from its inevitable destiny is like trying to stop a moth from breaking free of its cocoon.

Beloved friends in the practice need, above all, to be completely honest with each other, and such honesty takes great courage (courage being both eminently and etymologically a condition of *le coeur,* the heart). The whole parade of feelings, the lighthearted ones as well as the dark reflections, needs to be shared openly and honestly. Protecting your friend from his or her feelings of fear does not help your beloved find the courage needed to give birth to himself or herself.

First loves are always special and, at the time, feel as though they could never ever be replaced. But much later in his life an older and wiser Rumi could declare:

> He who came in a red frock in years past,
> He came this year in a brown garb.
> The Turk about whom you heard that time,
> Appeared as Arab this year.
>
> The friend is one, only the dress changes.
> He exchanged the garb and returned to me
>   again!
> The wine is one, only the bottles are different.
> How beautifully does this wine intoxicate us!

For the practitioner in the way of love, every loss of love is an invitation, a summoning to the next lover that it's time to appear. Every partner in the practice of gazing at the beloved adds a new adornment to the domain of union that the practice reveals. Rumi would come to understand this after Shams's death, first through his communion with the goldsmith Salahoddin, and later with his last great friend, Hosamoddin, the love of whom inspired Rumi to recite his great spiritual epic, the *Mathnavi*. In his later years, when he had the opportunity to reminisce about the similarities and differences in his relationships with his beloved friends, he would say that while Shams had been like the sun, burning relentlessly bright, Salahoddin had possessed the quality of the moon, gentle and soft, and Hosamoddin had been like a star, a twinkling muse and inspiration.

Had Shams not left Rumi when he did, had he stayed at his

side for the remainder of his days, there would have been the great likelihood that Rumi would have continued to revere Shams as the embodiment of God on Earth. While such devotion can be inspiring, it can also become a great obstacle to realization. Furthermore, it can falsely empower the teacher who is surrounded by adoring students and falsely disempower the students who never believe that they could possibly attain the stature of their teacher. Clearly, Shams didn't want this to happen. The purpose of the practices is for everyone to attain the royal throne of union.

Had Shams not left, Rumi's deepest layer of feelings may have never come unsprung. Grief has its own blessings, and if we could only accept and understand this, we would make our journey through life a lot easier to bear. Gradually, Rumi was able to let go of his obsession with Shams. Through opening himself again to others, he experienced the fire of freedom that Shams had been trying to ignite in him:

> *You moan, "She left me." "He left me."*
> *Quit your complaint.*
> *Twenty more will come.*

If you are going through a period of heartbreak, these words will be of little consolation. They can be spoken only after you've surfaced from your ordeal. While you're in the middle of your heartache, you need to be in the pain and feel the immeasurable loss, the awful certainty that what you want most from life has just been taken from you forever. This period is like the leavening time when the dough needs to sit undisturbed in a dark place and rise from within. Don't do yourself the disservice of thinking that there is anything shameful about undergoing such an ordeal. Bread that hasn't risen remains flat and tasteless.

How you go through your period of heartbreak is up to you. For the sweetness of love to open the heart, you have to be open to love's possibilities and accept its feelings. The same is true for heartbreak if it is to be of any benefit at all. If you stay closed to its wrenching feelings, you may miss its purifying fire. You may remain stuck in the cool shadows, projecting your hurt out onto your former lover in the form of blame and recrimination. Such projection can go on forever. It's like being in a bad dream from which you never awaken. Before you know it, your life may have passed you by.

If you've never had your heart broken, you've probably not yet fully entered into the path of love, and so the prophet Muhammad tells us:

> The earth and the sand are burning. Put your face on the burning sand and on the earth of the road, since all those who are wounded by love must have the imprint on their face, and the scar must be seen. Let the scar of the heart be seen, for by their scars are known the men who are in the way of love.

Practitioners on the path of love need to express their truths in whole, the beautiful revelations as well as the disturbing tugs and pulls, the felicities and torments alike, honestly and openly. In any case truth is right there, written large on their faces, for all the world to see.

Practitioners on the path of love never need to "save face." Why would they? The salvation that they seek is much deeper than any mask of ourselves that we may want to present to the world. An honest pain has a beauty to it. A false smile is ugly because it's unearned. Practitioners on the path of love never need to have cosmetic surgery to hide the life histories that appear as lines and wrinkles on the face. They seek a deeper beauty, a deeper radiance. To be among the privileged who view the rising of the sun in the land of union, they've had to stay up all night, never knowing if dawn would ever come.

The good news, as everyone who has undergone a dark night of heartache eventually learns, is that the dawn always comes. And when it does, you feel cured, just as meat that is marinated in bitter spices and slowly smoked becomes cured. Such a cure involves healing and maturation both. If a beloved suddenly leaves, a beloved to whom you risked opening your heart totally without playing it safe or guarding against a potential fall, you will cry your tears over the immeasurable loss. But you will also know that you were granted a privilege and ushered onto a path that more cautious people never get anywhere near. Rumi tells us to risk everything for love, that it is dangerous not to do so, and he tells us this even though he went through a heartbreak of mythical proportions.

Everyone has a deep spiritual longing in his or her heart, a deep yearning for completion. That longing will spur you on to find another with whom you can enter into the practices and go home to God; it will also torment you as months and years go by with no sign of that other's appearance. Never protect yourself from that longing, no matter how deep a hole it burns in your heart, for the longing you feel is God's way of making sure you never forget that your ultimate purpose is to find your way back to union. The longing in your heart is the ground of being as it attempts to give birth to itself through you. To join your soul with the soul of another, even if only for a brief moment, is worth whatever price you may be asked to pay.

II

Meeting the Friend

We all want a friend, but meeting someone who is to become the apple of our eye is not so easy as marching down to the corner grocery store and selecting a piece of fruit from a bin. Friends enter our life through grace, and the direct creation of grace is beyond our powers. All we can profitably do is to purify ourselves in anticipation of grace's arrival. Indeed, it is the commitment to purification, in combination with the longing in our hearts, that sets the winds of grace in motion and begins to summon the friend.

Don't think that you can sit around idly, biding your time until your friend shows up in your life, before you embark on your path of practices. No friend is going to accept your invitation for an extended visit until you first have your house in order. Take advantage of the time when you're on your own to do the practices that will prepare you for the shock of meeting the friend. Then, when the friend finally appears (having also been ardently doing his or her preparation practices in anticipation of finding you), you will both be prepared for the meeting.

Can a man who longs for a woman to complete him really believe that he needs to do nothing more than lose himself in television sports and drink imported beer while he's waiting for his beloved to appear? If he then walked into a room, his head filled with alcohol and his mind distracted by home run statistics, and Parvati herself were standing there, would she really be attracted to him? If you truly want a friend with whom to enter into the practices, then work to become the best that you are on your own, a person with whom an angel of God would want to associate. For your beloved friend will become like an angel to you, as you will to him or her. However, if you don't properly prepare yourself for a meeting of this magnitude, you may miss it entirely when it appears. The perfect friend may walk right past you, and you may not even notice:

> *In order to see you,*
> *Your face, your eyes,*
> *One must first clean the surface*
> *Of the heart's mirror with love.*

Prepare yourself by continually cleaning the surface and depths of your heart, and commit yourself to a disciplined practice.

When you enter into the practice of gazing at the beloved, the awareness of your body is going to be greatly magnified, so it's best to prepare and strengthen yourself in advance. Let the teachings of ma'iyya guide you as you move about in your life. Remember that God is to be found not just in your mind or in your heart, but in every little part and cell and atom of your body. So, whatever you're doing, wherever you are, keep remembering to bring your attention back to the sensations of your body. At every moment, on every part of your body, sensations can be felt to exist. Feel them. Surrender to them. Keep relaxing the body as much as you can, for tension makes it difficult to feel the sensations and energies that lie underneath.

Prepare yourself for the practice of gazing at your beloved friend by first familiarizing yourself with the experience of gazing at a variety of more neutral objects. Spend an entire hour sitting and gazing at the flame of a candle. Do this again and again. The candle's flame, like your friend's face, is always changing and flickering. When a thought appears and your mind wanders away from its one-pointed focus on the candle, relax the body, and simply bring your attention back to the flame. After a while, you will begin to experience a feeling of merging with the candle, as though you and the candle were entering into a shared dimension of experience. This may be your first taste of the realm of union. Enjoy it.

Union can appear only if you spend time looking for it. Ordinarily, we glance at an object and then move on to the next one. Spend time with a single object, relaxing your whole body as you gaze upon it. Certain forms of art such as Hindu yantras, Byzantine icons, Tibetan *thangka* paintings, or Buddhist *kasinas* (small discs of color) are designed to solicit your gaze, concentrate your mind, and give you a taste of union. The images relax your vision and invite you into communing with them. Don't just examine the individual features of these pieces of art, scanning their surfaces like a detective searching for clues to a crime. Look at the whole piece. See it all at once. Enter into the work of art, and let it penetrate you in return. The longer you look at these objects, the more they will escort you into the domain of union.

Finally, spend time gazing at your own face in a mirror. Sit in an upright sitting posture for an hour a day, relaxing your body and vision, gazing at your own reflection. Let your own eyes be the central object of your attention. Keep surrendering to the shifts in visual and tactile perception that will inevitably occur. Join seeing and seen together as one experience. If you do this every day for at least three months, the way you see will be irreversibly affected. As you continue to do this practice, you will become ever more adept at monitoring the relative tension and relaxation you feel in your eyes. You will also experience how the relaxation of your vision leads to union, while tension leads to involuntary thought and the alienated feeling of separation. Your ability to stay relaxed in the gaze and to have your eyes remain calm and still will increase. Most important, you will nurture a steadiness and energy in your gaze that another person, with the eyes to see, will be able to recognize:

> *Give the beautiful ones mirrors*
> *And let them fall in love with themselves.*
> *That way they polish their souls*
> *And kindle remembering in others.*

It's not just a physical beauty that draws you to the beloved friend. It's an inner presence as well—an inner radiance. Sometimes, the friend in the practice who comes into your life may not look anything at all like the kind of person to whom you're ordinarily attracted. Trust your feelings and trust your eyes. Don't miss what's just arrived on your doorstep because you haven't cultivated enough vision to see it for what it is. Anyone can fall in love with a beautiful face only to realize, many months down the road, that there was much about this person that was somehow ignored or unnoticed at the initial meeting.

Practice seeing. Continually examine the relationship between the part of you that sees and the visual field onto which you look. Notice that when you're lost in thought, you lose your awareness of both bodily sensations and the visual field. All preliminary practices serve to help us learn how to be present in each moment—this moment—in the most relaxed way possible. There's never been a better time than right now to see and feel. And in the next moment, right now is again just as good, as it is in the next one and the next one still.

The more you can practice seeing and feeling, perhaps formally in a sitting meditation practice, perhaps informally as you move about in your life, the better prepared you will be when the one you have been seeking finally appears. Moreover, the ability to see and feel generates a palpable energy with a strong field of influence; this field of energy will help draw your friend to you.

Throughout his poetry Rumi keeps referring, over and over again, to two other specific practices that can powerfully support the practitioner on the path of love. Both help prepare a person's body for the shock to the system that inevitably occurs when the beloved appears, and both help to keep the body healthy and the mind fluid during the commingling with the beloved.

The first of these practices is the periodic withdrawal of food through fasting:

> *Try to obtain the eyes which see God*
> *Through the eyesight of fasting.*

Food is the addictive drug of choice in Western culture. We are all like the caricature of the Mexican laborer who wisely takes a siesta after his heavy midday meal. The purpose of the practice of gazing at the beloved, however, is not to enter into a soothing slumber, but to wake up to the reality of union. To be hungry and in need of food is a terrible thing, but to overeat because of the abundance of food that's available is one of the guaranteed ways to stay forever domiciled in the land of separation. Learning to eat nutritiously and lightly is one of the cornerstones on which good physical health is built, and practitioners on the path of love must keep their bodies healthy and strong. Even fat and happy Buddhas have likely undergone periods in which they temporarily refrained from eating.

Food isn't all that nourishes the practitioner on the path of love:

> *Don't eat too much of the food*
> *That becomes a curtain over your eyes.*
> *If you do, you won't be able to find your way*
>   *back home.*

Although you think your life
Depends on this little morsel of food,
It's actually more like a hair
That has grown too long
And is covering over the eyes of your soul,
A curtain covering over your head's eye.

Too much food dulls the awareness of your bodily sensations and sets you dreamily adrift in your mind. When you eat lightly, however, it becomes much easier to feel the full range of the body's sensations and to yield to the pulls and currents that draw two friends in the practice together into union. Eating lightly turns food for the body into food for the soul, and powerfully stimulates the practice of gazing at the beloved.

Just as you want to decrease the amount of food that you routinely take into your body and to undergo periodic fasting, so too do you want to increase the amount of oxygen that you inhale with each breath. Surrendering to the cleansing power of the breath is the second technique to which Rumi constantly refers in his writings. A full and natural breath blows you to the shore of union while a restricted and shallow breath will tie you up at the dock of separation:

Just as wind is under God's command,
So is breath under yours.
Breath can either curse loudly or sing praises.
It all depends on you.

The condition of your body is a direct reflection of the condition of your breath. If your breath is shallow and restricted, you will have only a very limited awareness of the sensations of your body, but if your breath is naturally full and free, then your body will be filled with vibrant sensations, and the principle of ma'iyya will be self-evident.

One of the most effective ways you have to practice surrender to God is to give in, as much as possible, to each and every breath you take. You can turn your back on the energies of God, but you can never completely banish their controlling influence in your life. So too can you diminish the force of the breath you allow into your body, but you can never ever stop breathing until it is time for you to leave this world. Surrendering to each and every breath gives birth to God through your body, over and over and yet over again:

> See how you can bring new Soul
> Into every breath you take
> And turn into the Messiah.
> When your soul becomes cleansed
> In each breath you breathe,
> You will understand
> How Jesus was born from every breath.

Just as you can train yourself to remain aware of the full range of sensations that you feel in your body, so too can you learn to feel the full force of your breath moving through your entire body from head to foot. When you truly relax and surrender your will, your breath naturally explodes open. Instead of your lungs and diaphragm, your whole body then becomes your organ of respiration, just as your whole body can be experienced as your organ of vision.

From time to time during the day, as often as you possibly can, remember to examine your breath. Feel how the holding and tension in your body interfere with the free flow of breath. Relax the holding and tension and see how your breath immediately opens and becomes fuller. Feel the entire range of sensations that exist in your body right now, and then join your awareness of breathing to the feeling-presence of your entire body.

Life is a journey that you ride on your breath, from your first inhalation to your last exhalation. Unfurl the sail of your body, and let your breath fill you from head to foot and guide you on your way. Feel how this powerful, yet completely natural and unforced breath wants to fill your sails and move through your whole body, massaging sensations into wakefulness as it passes over them.

Prepare yourself well for meeting your friend. Prepare your body and mind as best you can for the encounter that you're drawing to yourself. Use this time wisely. Do sitting practices in front of a mirror. Practice gazing at a candle or a piece of sacred art. Eat lightly. Bring your awareness to your full range of bodily sensations and the fullest expression of your breath. Remain mindful of the sounds, sights, and sensations of this moment as you move about in your life. And keep your heart open as much as you possibly can. You never know when the beloved is going to show up. It is this passion and dedication, combined with the longing you feel for the beloved who hasn't yet appeared, that will draw him or her to you.

> *Work. Keep digging your well.*
> *Don't think about getting off from work.*
> *Water is there somewhere.*
>
> *Submit to a daily practice.*
> *Your loyalty to that*
> *Is a ring on the door.*
>
> *Keep knocking, and the joy inside*
> *Will eventually open a window*
> *And look out to see who's there.*

When the beloved finally knocks on your door, when suddenly the friend appears, standing innocently in front of you, welcome him or her immediately with open arms and heart. When, through the perfect mixture of preparation and grace, someone comes to you and you are both drawn into the practice, acknowledge your great good fortune. Honor and respect your friend, because nothing in the world can compare to the wonderment of this encounter:

> When the ocean finally comes to you as a lover,
> Marry, at once, quickly,
> For God's sake!
>
> Don't postpone it!
> Existence has no better gift.
> No amount of searching
> Will find this.
>
> A perfect falcon, for no reason,
> has landed on your shoulder,
> And become yours.

What brings two friends in the practice together? It's that something in each soul needs something in the other soul in order to grow and evolve. What, then, are friends for? First and foremost, friends are permission givers, offering each other complete permission to be themselves. What a blessing to relax completely in the presence of another! By feeling fully accepted by your friend, you feel safe to accept yourself more fully. Real friendship always requires a deep surrender to the mixing of souls that the friendship has brought into being. Two friends bring out what's inside each other and protect the easement that takes them both into the world of union. Through this shared trust, friends give each other what they desire the most:

> At last I have found what patience can bring,
> This one whose face can answer any question,

Who simply by looking can loosen the knot of
  intellectual discussion.
You translate what is inside us.
If you were to vanish,
This vast meeting room would shrink to a closet.
Protect us.

While you can profitably explore the practice of gazing at the beloved with anyone, you'll feel much more of an attraction to enter into it with some people over others. Eventually, someone may come into your life that you feel so magnetically drawn to that all you want is to do the practice with him or her. Until that time comes, continue to do your preparation, explore the practice informally with as many people as possible, and trust in the ultimate matchmaking skills of God. The person that you most need to encounter in your life may be knocking at your door right now.

Don't turn someone away because he or she doesn't match your perfect pictures of what a beloved friend should look and act like. At the same time, don't settle for a lesser relationship than you deserve. We all crave connection and long for completion. Keep as a constant prayer in your heart your burning desire to meet your friend. That's what Shams did, and finally his prayer was answered and he made his way to Konya:

If you don't have a beloved,
Why don't you go out and search for one?
If you've reached the beloved,
Why don't you rejoice and sing praises?

O, one who has reached maturity,
Choose another mature one.
Stay next to him.

Go together to the land of timelessness and
spacelessness.
To avoid that is to make a big mistake.

As human beings, we have but three requirements in life: food, shelter, and someone to love and be loved by. If we have these three, then our journey through life can be a journey of riches. Everything else is filler. When queried as to their hopes for their twilight years, most people reply that they hope for a comfortable life and someone to share it with. Only rarely do we come across anyone who hopes to remove himself or herself completely from the social fabric of life and live alone in a cave.

We're all on a journey back home to God. The only unknown is whether we'll experience that homecoming while we're still alive in our physical body or enter into it when we die. Meeting the friend, with all the joys and heartaches that may entail, can help move you along on your journey so that you can live your passion here and now.

So do whatever it takes to find your friend. Play together. Bathe in the practice together. Explore this most consummate of mysteries together. Find out what it means, no, what it *feels like* to be human, what it feels like to be fully alive, what it feels like to be one with a friend.

Afterword

S o, what do you think? Is this not what the beloved friends Jalaluddin and Shams were doing together? But, please, don't take my word for it. Find out for yourself. Sit down with your friend and explore the practice together. Like the original Biblical birthright, Joseph's coat of many colors, try it on for size. See how it fits. See how wearing it affects you, how it changes you forever, how it transforms you back into yourself.

If you believe what has been written here but don't dive into the warm waters of the practice, swim and loll and splash to your heart's content, then you may have resolved in your mind the mystery of what Jalaluddin and Shams were doing together behind the closed doors of their retreat room, but you will still be no closer to resolving the great mystery that besets your own heart.

If you don't believe what has been presented here . . . well, that's fine too. My primary purpose in writing this book was not to be acknowledged as the person who finally figured out the solution to a centuries-old riddle, but to present a wonderful set of practices that you and your friend can enter into right now, today. All I would ask of you who don't believe (or who feel that anyone who presumes to have even an inkling of what Jalaluddin and Shams might have been up to should be branded and dismissed as too impertinent) is this: find a friend, and be with him or her for forty days and nights, surrendering totally to the practices and to all the frictions and meltings and mixings that they generate. If you still don't believe, then I might be more inclined to listen to you; but know that real friendship erases doubt and makes believers out of even the most jaundiced souls.

So exquisite are his words that there exists the very real danger that Rumi may become one of those teachers whose sayings are revered but whose practices are not followed. Feast on his words. Savor each and every one. Let them whet your spiritual appetite, tantalize your spiritual taste buds, tease you into acknowledging what you know you want more than anything but are perhaps too reticent to admit. But don't stop there. His words can incite you to fill your spiritual belly, but they can't satisfy the hunger that lies therein. Only if you take his words literally to heart and enter into the practices will you understand what he's truly telling you. And you'll understand not just through the joy of your mind that delights in the elegant play of words and images, but with every deep fiber of your soul.

As was discussed earlier, the long tradition within Sufism of the power of the gaze has involved isolated events, particular occasions in which a powerful being casts his or her glance and lets it fall on someone. The reception of such a glance has been likened to parched earth receiving life-giving rain. What Rumi and Shams did that was so radical and revolutionary was to take this isolated event out of the vertical and hierarchical teacher-student relationship and turn it on its side, making it into a prolonged practice and mutual exploration between two friends. No longer is there a gazer in the role of teacher and a gazed upon in the role of student. Now there are only friends, dancing and whirling through the progressive stages of a prolonged and mutual gaze.

Such a radical shift in how spiritual teachings are to be transmitted accords precisely with Buddhist legends about the coming of the next Buddha. The historical Buddha was always addressed as Bhagwan, which means the holy one as teacher, but the coming Buddha will be known simply as Maitreya, the friend. In a more egalitarian world, all friends who enter into relationship with each other become themselves the source through which teachings can be most effectively transmitted, revealed, and received. There are teachers on the planet today who still sit at the front of the room and have their students gaze at them. How much more powerful it would be if they would have their students turn to gaze at one another instead.

Even though the practice of gazing at the beloved apparently was never shared within the wider Sufi world as a formal practice, it kept resurfacing from time to time, here and there, wherever people had the eyes to see and the ears to hear and the good fortune to stumble across the teachings. A century after Rumi, for example, the Sufi poet Hafiz would write:

> There is a game we should play,
> And it goes like this:
>
> We hold hands and look into each other's eyes
> And scan each other's face.
>
> Then I say,
> "Now, tell me a difference between us."
>
> And you might respond,
> "Hafiz, your nose is ten times bigger than mine!"
>
> Then I would say,
> "Yes, my dear, almost ten times!"

But let's keep playing,
Let's go deeper,
Go deeper.
For if we do,
Our spirits will embrace
And interweave.

Our union will be so glorious
That even God
Will not be able to tell us apart.

There is a wonderful game
We should play with everyone
And it goes like this. . . .

The practice of gazing at the beloved, this sharing of energy and mixing together of souls, is a wonderful game, but it's fundamentally different from the other wonderful games we enjoy playing. Don't think that it's like Monopoly with its competition and harsh rules such as, "go directly to jail, do not pass Go, do not collect two hundred dollars." Just the opposite is true. Winning in this game is business as *un*usual. It has nothing to do with monopolizing everything and sending your fellow players to the poorhouse in the process. It's all about having everyone win. It's all about merging with another. It's about springing the energies of God from their imprisonment within the human body. It's about going, going, going completely gone and receiving incredible riches of soul for your efforts.

The longing you feel in your heart is the ground of union itself calling you to hold the gaze of a beloved friend. Whenever two people come together in relationship and truly surrender to their deepest nature, they cannot help but look at each other and enter into the practice, whether they know about it or not. The magnetism of the ground of union draws their eyes together every bit as powerfully as a paper clip is drawn across the surface of a table by a magnet. When you enter into the practice, you are simply surrendering to a law of nature; if you don't know about this law it's only because the world of separation has so resisted acknowledging its simple truth.

Do you remember how great a joy it was when, as a child, you played with your first magnet? For long hours, you remained mesmerized as the clips and pins and iron filings leapt across the table and embraced the magnet. As an adult, let the practice of gazing at the beloved magnetize and mesmerize you in the same way. A soul leaps across empty space and becomes reunited with its heart's desire. How can it possibly be!? Wouldn't you like to find out? Well, it's all very easy really. There's a wonderful game we can play, and it goes like this. . . .

If you wish to communicate with the author, please address your correspondence to will@embodiment.net or the Institute for Embodiment Training, 6688 Grandview Road, Duncan, B.C. V9L 5Y7, Canada. For information about programs based on the principles outlined in this book, peruse the website at www.embodiment.net.

Shhhh. No more words.
Hear only the voice within.

Acknowledgments

First of all, I want to thank the many gifted translators and poets who've brought Rumi to the English-speaking world and who've made him the most popular poet in the world today: A. J. Arberry and Nevit O. Ergin, Robert Bly and Coleman Barks, Andrew Harvey, Kabir Helminski, Sharam Shiva, and James Cowan among others.

Many years ago, as a young man, while wrestling with the experiences that the practice was revealing to me, I began searching through the spiritual literature in hopes of finding some mention of a lineage—anything that might help reassure me that the path I had accidentally stumbled upon was leading not to greater confusion but to greater wisdom. On the very first page of the very first Rumi book that I ever opened I found exactly what I was looking for.

Early on in the writing of this book, I realized that I needed to befriend a Rumi scholar to help guide me in my work. Imagine my utter surprise and delight when I went into a bookstore and picked from the shelf *Signs of the Unseen,* a translation of Rumi's discourses, only to realize that the author, W. M. Thackston Jr. of Harvard University, was an old friend of mine from undergraduate days at Princeton! Thank you, Wheeler, for all the reading and rereading that you've done, for your patience in answering my endless lists of questions, for our correspondence about shad roe and bird's nests, and for all your encouragement and support.

Emily Sell of Shambhala Publications, in addition to being the editor for several of my books, has become over the years one of my dearest friends, supporters, confidantes, and even a partner in the practice. We share with each other an equal fascination in the challenge of expressing through words what words alone can never describe, this great domain of the heart and soul. It was Emily who first suggested that I write a book about the gazing practice, and it was Emily who encouraged me to read as much of Rumi's writings as I could get my hands on to determine if my hunch that he and Shams were engaged in the gazing practice was, in fact, accurate.

I'm extremely grateful to Jon Graham, the acquisitions editor of Inner Traditions, and to Jeanie Levitan, the managing editor, for their courage and vision in supporting this project. Of all the publishing houses who saw this book, it was Inner Traditions that truly understood the value and implications of what I'd done and who were not only willing, but excited to participate in a project that many more cautious people viewed as too controversial.

I would also like to make special mention of Laura Schlivek, my exceedingly thoughtful project editor at Inner Traditions, and Dana Walsh, my copy editor. Copy editors in particular are the unsung heroes of the publishing industry, and Dana's contribution has gone far beyond matters of syntax and grammar, making this a much more enjoyable book for you to read.

Most of all, I want to thank the many friends and consorts in the practice who've come into my life and who've taught me so much: Phil, whose generosity in stopping to pick me up hitchhiking on a street corner in Berkeley changed my life; Joka (Ma Ananda Kavita), who had been introduced to the practice during long private visits with a young Bhagwan Shree Rajneesh in the 1960s in Bombay and whom I look upon as my Shams; Sue, a night owl who nevertheless, and without complaint, always accepted that my punctual ten o'clock yawns signaled that it was time to let me go to sleep; Jack Downing and Lyn (in the world of Argentine tango at which she excels, invitations to the dance are never expressed in words, but only through eye contact!), who told me of Oscar Ichazo's approach to the practice; my son Kailas, who engaged me as deeply in the practice as I've ever gone just one minute after he was born (who could have known that twenty years to the day after that event I would finish this manuscript?!); Ali (Fish), who brought happiness and wealth back into my life; Carla (Crow), who forced me to find the gold that lies buried over in them thar' hills of heartbreak; all of the many students and friends I've met through my affiliation with the Institute for Embodiment Training.

For many years now, Bob Nelford has remained my primary male friend in the practice. Shams needed to find someone to endure his company, and Bob has mostly managed to tolerate mine. The same inner voice that comes to me during my practices and helps me to understand further how this all works comes to him now as well. We start and finish each other's sentences, and many of them have made their way into this book.

And, finally, there's Courtenay (Pony), proof positive that angels sometimes speak with a hint of a Fort Worth drawl. It was you who showed up. It was you who God sent through my door. It was you who said yes, who always, without hesitation, kept saying yes, and who summoned me to respond in kind, in love, and through that response (what else could we do?!) we became funnels through which we poured ourselves into God.

May this book serve as an invitation and call to the tribe of gazers to reassemble and find one another once again. *Svaha!*

References for Rumi's Poetry and Discourses

Sources for all the Rumi quotations used in this book are listed as follows. Quotations are listed by chapter, and the first line of each quotation is cited for easy reference. Where the author has reworded an existing English translation, mention of this rewording and the original source from which it derives are both cited. We have created abbreviated references for the works most frequently cited. The abbreviations are as follows:

ER — Coleman Barks, *The Essential Rumi* (New York: HarperCollins, 1994).

MCR 7b — Nevit O. Ergin, *Mevlana Celaleddin Rumi, Divan-i Kebir, Meter 7b* (San Clemente, Calif.: Echo Publications, 1995).

Introduction

Look at me: Nevit O. Ergin, MCR 7b.

Chapter 1: Jalaluddin and Shams

Oh, Shams of Tabriz: Andrew Harvey, *Song of the Sun* (Boulder, Colo.: Sounds True, 1999).

Look through Shams' eyes: Coleman Barks, ER.

I said to him, "Your zeal is great,": my rewording of a passage from Nevit O. Ergin, MCR 7b.

The eye of the sea is one thing: Andrew Harvey, *Teachings of Rumi* (Boston: Shambhala, 1999).

Know that with your departure my mind and faith have been stripped: James Cowan, *Rumi's Divan of Shems of Tabriz* (Rockport, Mass.: Element, 1997).

O my Beauty, I have fallen in Your love: Nevit O. Ergin, *Mevlana Celaleddin Rumi, Divan-i Kebir, Meter 8b* (Los Angeles: Echo Publications, 1998).

A saint went on a retreat: my rewording of a passage from W. M. Thackston Jr., *Signs of the Unseen* (Boston: Shambhala, 1994).

Both our sets of eyes became drunk: my rewording of a passage from Nevit O. Ergin, MCR 7b.

Now, what shall we call this new sort of gazing house: Coleman Barks, ER.

Chapter 2: The Two Worlds and the Lover's Resolution

Behind this world opens an infinite universe: Andrew Harvey, *Teachings of Rumi* (Boston: Shambhala, 1999).

Everything you see has its roots in the unseen world: Andrew Harvey, *Song of the Sun* (Boulder, Colo.: Sounds True, 1999).

A corporeal being has such power: W. M. Thackston Jr., *Signs of the Unseen* (Boston: Shambhala, 1994).

I would rather see my friends: W. M. Thackston Jr., *Signs of the Unseen* (Boston: Shambhala, 1994).

Infinite mercy flows continually: Andrew Harvey, *Teachings of Rumi* (Boston: Shambhala, 1999).

The way of the mind is discussion, inquiry: Nevit O. Ergin, MCR 7b.

There is no solution for the soul but to fall in love: Andrew Harvey, *Song of the Sun* (Boulder, Colo.: Sounds True, 1999).

Wherever you are: W. M. Thackston Jr., *Signs of the Unseen* (Boston: Shambhala, 1994).

The way you make love is the way: Coleman Barks, ER.

At breakfast, a lover asked her lover, as a test: Andrew Harvey, *Teachings of Rumi* (Boston: Shambhala, 1999).

May anyone who says, "Save him from love!": Andrew Harvey, *Teachings of Rumi* (Boston: Shambhala, 1999).

Chapter 3: Body of Separation, Body of Union

Although the light of soul is essential: Nevit O. Ergin, MCR.

The most important dance is the one that happens inside us: Nevit O. Ergin, *Mevlana Celaleddin Rumi, Divan-i Kebir, Meter 8a* (Los Angeles: Echo Publications, 1998).

I have no idea whether I am a bright soul: Nevit O. Ergin, MCR 7b.

Inside your body is a priceless treasure: Nevit O. Ergin, *Mevlana Celaleddin Rumi, Divan-i Kebir, Meter 8b* (Los Angeles: Echo Publications, 1998).

The body is a device to calculate: Coleman Barks, ER.

The snow says all the time: Annemarie Schimmel, *I Am Wind, You Are Fire* (Boston: Shambhala Publications, 1992).

The work of religion is nothing but astonishment: Andrew Harvey, *Teachings of Rumi* (Boston: Shambhala, 1999).

So he speaks, and everyone around him: Coleman Barks, ER.

A sweet voice came: Nevit O. Ergin, MCR 7b.

The body is a mirror of heaven: Andrew Harvey, *The Way of Passion* (Berkeley: Frog, Ltd., 1994).

Chapter 4: Gazing at the Beloved

Friend sits by Friend: Coleman Barks, ER.

Look as long as you can at the friend you love: Coleman Barks, ER.

Come to the sea of charm and beauty: my rewording of a passage from Nevit O. Ergin, MCR 7b.

Dive into the sea which is full of glory: Nevit O. Ergin, MCR 7b.

If there are hundreds of curtains: Nevit O. Ergin, *Mevlana Celaleddin Rumi, Divan-i Kebir, Meter 3* (Lake Isabella, Calif.: Echo Publications, 1995).

Every particle of my body: my rewording of a passage from Nevit O. Ergin, *Mevlana Celaleddin Rumi, Divan-i Kebir, Meter 8a* (Los Angeles: Echo Publications, 1998).

Thousands of times I ran away from you: Nevit O. Ergin, MCR 7b.

Acceptance is the key to happiness: Andrew Harvey, *Song of the Sun* (Boulder, Colo.: Sounds True, 1999).

You suppose that you're the trouble: Nevit O. Ergin, MCR 7b.

We are like bowls floating on the surface of water: W. M. Thackston Jr., *Signs of the Unseen* (Boston: Shambhala, 1994).

Why have you turned into a dry branch: Nevit O. Ergin, MCR 7b.

The glowing eyes of this doctor dispense remedies: Nevit O. Ergin, MCR 7b.

He said to me, "Why are your eyes so fixed on my face?": Andrew Harvey, *Teachings of Rumi* (Boston: Shambhala, 1999).

Borrow the beloved's eyes: Coleman Barks, ER.

My soul dissolves in you, and with you is mingled: Coleman Barks, ER.

You knock at the door of reality: Coleman Barks, ER.

The beauty of Love is the merger: Nevit O. Ergin, MCR 7b.

Whenever two are linked this way: Coleman Barks, ER.

If He is not in your eye: Nevit O. Ergin, MCR 7b.

I became totally eyes from head to feet: Nevit O. Ergin, *Mevlana Celaleddin Rumi, Divan-i Kebir, Meter 3* (Lake Isabella, Calif.: Echo Publications, 1995).

The mystery does not get clearer by repeating the question: Coleman Barks, ER.

What disguises he wears, what tricks he invents!: James Cowan, *Rumi's Divan of Shems of Tabriz* (Rockport, Mass.: Element, 1997).

When his bright face becomes an eye: Nevit O. Ergin, MCR 7b.

You turned into eyes: Nevit O. Ergin, MCR 7b.

For God's sake, don't ask for the taste: Nevit O. Ergin, *Mevlana Celaleddin Rumi, Divan-i Kebir, Meter 8b* (Los Angeles: Echo Publications, 1998).

Nobody but the blind asks me: Nevit O. Ergin, MCR 7b.

The one you call crazy: my rewording of a passage from Nevit O. Ergin, *Mevlana Celaleddin Rumi, Divan-i Kebir, Meter 3* (Lake Isabella, Calif.: Echo Publications, 1995).

The beauty of that Arab caught my mind and my heart: Nevit O. Ergin, MCR 7b.

Both our eyes became drunk with the glass: my rewording of a passage from Nevit O. Ergin, MCR 7b.

The patron of your eyes is God: Nevit O. Ergin, MCR 7b.

The importance of eye and sight: Nevit O. Ergin, MCR 7b.

Look at the drunken eyes of the person: Nevit O. Ergin, MCR 7b.

His soul is a mirror that reflects the beauty of God: my rewording of a passage from Nevit O. Ergin, *Mevlana Celaleddin Rumi, Divan-i Kebir, Meter 4* (Lake Isabella, Calif.: Echo Publications, 1996).

We are looking at your face: my rewording of a passage from Nevit O. Ergin, *Mevlana Celaleddin Rumi, Divan-i Kebir, Meter 4* (Lake Isabella, Calif.: Echo Publications, 1996).

My eyes have wet dreams: Nevit O. Ergin, *Mevlana Celaleddin Rumi, Divan-i Kebir, Meter 4* (Lake Isabella, Calif.: Echo Publications, 1996).

Chapter 5: Language of the Heart

Be silent: This poem is taken from three separate passages from Nevit O. Ergin, *Mevlana Celaleddin Rumi, Divan-i Kebir, Meter 4* (Lake Isabella, Calif.: Echo Publications, 1996) and from Nevit O. Ergin, *Mevlana Celaleddin Rumi, Divan-i Kebir, Meter 2* (Sun Valley, Calif.: Echo Publications, 1995).

All our lives we've looked: Coleman Barks, ER.

Even "friend" and "beloved": Coleman Barks, *The Glance* (New York: Viking Penguin, 1999).

In the silence of our longing: Nevit O. Ergin, *Mevlana Celaleddin Rumi, Divan-i Kebir, Meter 3* (Lake Isabella, Calif.: Echo Publications, 1995).

You have spent your whole life: Nevit O. Ergin, *Mevlana Celaleddin Rumi, Divan-i Kebir, Meter 2* (Sun Valley, Calif.: Echo Publications, 1995).

What would happen if you: Nevit O. Ergin, *Mevlana Celaleddin Rumi, Divan-i Kebir, Meter 2* (Sun Valley, Calif.: Echo Publications, 1995).

Thought doesn't come to your mind: my rewording of a passage from Nevit O. Ergin, *Mevlana Celaleddin Rumi, Divan-i Kebir, Meter 2* (Sun Valley, Calif.: Echo Publications, 1995).

The Prince rides forth to hunt in the morning: James Cowan, *Rumi's Divan of Shems of Tabriz* (Rockport, Mass.: Element, 1997).

Tell my secret with your eyes: Nevit O. Ergin, *Mevlana Celaleddin Rumi, Divan-i Kebir, Meter 8b* (Los Angeles: Echo Publications, 1998).

Every moment a new fountain springs from the heart: Nevit O. Ergin, *Mevlana Celaleddin Rumi, Divan-i Kebir, Meter 8b* (Los Angeles: Echo Publications, 1998).

Either give me wine or leave me alone: Coleman Barks, ER.

I know I ought to be silent: Coleman Barks, ER.

I think of rhymes, but my beloved says: Annemarie Schimmel, *The Triumphal Sun* (Albany, N.Y.: State University of New York Press, 1978).

I have seen your unseeable beauty: my rewording of a passage from Coleman Barks, *The Glance* (New York: Viking Penguin, 1999).

My drunken eyes: my rewording of a passage from Nevit O. Ergin, *Mevlana Celaleddin Rumi, Divan-i Kebir, Meter 4* (Lake Isabella, Calif.: Echo Publications, 1996).

Chapter 6: The Birthing River of Darkness and Light

An unseen well can be found: my rewording of a passage from Nevit O. Ergin, *Mevlana Celaleddin Rumi, Divan-i Kebir, Meter 8a* (Los Angeles: Echo Publications, 1998).

If the sun wouldn't go behind: Nevit O. Ergin, MCR 7b.

As long as Mary did not feel the pain of childbirth: Andrew Harvey, *The Way of Passion* (Berkeley: Frog, Ltd., 1994).

The man of heart has accepted everything: W. M. Thackston Jr., *Signs of the Unseen* (Boston: Shambhala, 1994).

This being human is a guest house: Coleman Barks, ER.

My head became drunk and passed out of itself: Nevit O. Ergin, *Mevlana Celaleddin Rumi, Divan-i Kebir, Meter 8b* (Los Angeles: Echo Publications, 1998).

You've endured many terrible griefs: Andrew Harvey, *Teachings of Rumi* (Boston: Shambhala, 1999).

Chapter 7: Laughter

It is impossible to hide a smile: Nevit O. Ergin, *Mevlana Celaleddin Rumi, Divan-i Kebir, Meter 3* (Lake Isabella, Calif.: Echo Publications, 1995).

I laugh not just with my mouth: Nevit O. Ergin, *Mevlana Celaleddin Rumi, Divan-i Kebir, Meter 3* (Lake Isabella, Calif.: Echo Publications, 1995).

Chapter 8: Friends and Consorts

Out beyond ideas of wrong doing and right doing: The source of this quotation was not cited, but appeared in Michele Cassou and Stewart Cubley, *Life, Paint and Passion* (New York: Jeremy P. Tarcher, 1994).

Chapter 9: Learning to See

If you want to know God: my rewording of a passage from Coleman Barks, ER.

Whenever you stop looking: Nevit O. Ergin, *Mevlana Celaleddin Rumi, Divan-i Kebir, Meter 4* (Lake Isabella, Calif.: Echo Publications, 1996).

Dissolve your whole body into Vision: The source of this quotation was not cited, but it appeared in D. E. Harding, *On Having No Head* (London: The Buddhist Society, 1961).

We are always and ever in communication: W. M. Thackston Jr., *Signs of the Unseen* (Boston: Shambhala, 1994).

Chapter 10: Heartbreak

Your cruel separation: Nevit O. Ergin, *Mevlana Celaleddin Rumi, Divan-i Kebir, Meter 2* (Sun Valley, Calif.: Echo Publications, 1996).

Your eyes every moment: my rewording of a passage from Nevit O. Ergin, *Mevlana Celaleddin Rumi, Divan-i Kebir, Meter 4* (Lake Isabella, Calif.: Echo Publications, 1996).

For lovers, to run away from the beloved: Nevit O. Ergin, *Mevlana Celaleddin Rumi, Divan-i Kebir, Meter 2* (Sun Valley, Calif.: Echo Publications, 1996).

Love is not the business of delicate people: Nevit O. Ergin, *Mevlana Celaleddin Rumi, Divan-i Kebir, Meter 8a* (Los Angeles: Echo Publications, 1998).

The body that drank this wine: Nevit O. Ergin, MCR 7b.

I am adding the water of cruelty to the honey of ecstasy: Nevit O. Ergin, MCR 7b.

He who came in a red frock in years past: Annemarie Schimmel, *The Triumphal Sun* (Albany, N.Y.: State University of New York Press, 1978).

You moan, "She left me." "He left me.": Coleman Barks, ER.

Chapter 11: Meeting the Friend

In order to see you: Nevit O. Ergin, MCR 7b.

Give the beautiful ones mirrors: Coleman Barks, ER.

Try to obtain the eyes which see God: Nevit O. Ergin, *Mevlana Celaleddin Rumi, Divan-i Kebir, Meter 3* (Lake Isabella, Calif.: Echo Publications, 1995).

Don't eat too much of the food: Nevit O. Ergin, MCR 7b.

Just as wind is under God's command: Nevit O. Ergin, *Mevlana Celaleddin Rumi, Divan-i Kebir, Meter 8b* (Los Angeles: Echo Publications, 1998).

See how you bring new soul: Nevit O. Ergin, *Mevlana Celaleddin Rumi, Divan-i Kebir, Meter 8b* (Los Angeles: Echo Publications, 1998).

Work. Keep digging your well: Coleman Barks, ER.

When the ocean finally comes to you as a lover: Coleman Barks, ER.

At last I have found what patience can bring: Coleman Barks, ER.

If you don't have a beloved: Nevit O. Ergin, MCR 7b.

O, one who has reached maturity: Nevit O. Ergin, *Mevlana Celaleddin Rumi, Divan-i Kebir, Meter 4* (Lake Isabella, Calif.: Echo Publications, 1996).

Afterword

Shhh. No more words: Jonathan Star and Shahram Shiva, *A Garden Beyond Paradise: Mystical Poetry of Rumi* (New York: Bantam Books, 1992).

Books of Related Interest

The Rubais of Rumi
Insane with Love
Translations and commentary by
Nevit O. Ergin and Will Johnson

The Forbidden Rumi
The Suppressed Poems of Rumi on Love,
Heresy, and Intoxication
Translations and commentary by
Nevit O. Ergin and Will Johnson

Yoga of the Mahamudra
The Mystical Way of Balance
by Will Johnson

The Sailfish and the Sacred Mountain
Passages in the Lives of a Father and Son
by Will Johnson

Journey to the Lord of Power
A Sufi Manual on Retreat
by Ibn Arabi, with commentary by Abd al-Kerim al-Jili
Translated from the Arabic by Rabia Terry Harris

The Way of Sufi Chivalry
by Ibn al-Husayn al-Sulami
An interpretation by Tosun Bayrak al-Jerrahi

The Book of Sufi Healing
by Shaykh Hakim Moinuddin Chishti

Haféz
Teachings of the Philosopher of Love
by Haleh Pourafzal and Roger Montgomery

Inner Traditions • Bear & Company
P.O. Box 388
Rochester, VT 05767
1-800-246-8648
www.InnerTraditions.com

Or contact your local bookseller